Guiding Those Left Behind
In Arizona

LEGAL AND PRACTICAL THINGS
YOU NEED TO DO
TO SETTLE AN ESTATE IN ARIZONA
and

HOW TO ARRANGE YOUR OWN AFFAIRS
TO AVOID UNNECESSARY COSTS
TO YOUR FAMILY

By AMELIA E. POHL, ESQ.

and Arizona Attorney
PAUL B. BARTLETT

 EAGLE PUBLISHING COMPANY OF BOCA

The purpose of this book is to provide the reader with an informative overview of the subject; but laws change frequently and are subject to different interpretations as courts rule on the meaning or effect of a law. This book is sold with the understanding that neither the authors, nor the editors, nor the publisher, nor the distributors of this book are engaging in, or rendering, legal, accounting, financial planning, or any other professional service. Pursuant to Internal Revenue Service guidance, be advised that any federal tax advice in this publication was not intended or written to be used, and it cannot be used, by any person or entity for the purpose of avoiding penalties imposed under the Internal Revenue Code (IRS Circular 230 Disclaimer). If you need legal, accounting, financial planning or any other expert advice, you should seek the services of a licensed professional.

This book is intended for use by the consumer for his or her own benefit. If you use this book to counsel someone about the law or tax matters, that may be considered to be an unlicensed and illegal practice.

WEB SITES: Web sites appear throughout the book for the convenience of the reader only. Publication of these Web site addresses is not an endorsement by the authors, editors or publishers of this book.

EAGLE PUBLISHING COMPANY OF BOCA
4199 N. Dixie Highway, #2
Boca Raton, FL   33431   E-mail: info@eaglepublishing.com

Printed in the United States of America   ISBN 1932464093
Library of Congress Catalog Card Number 2005822150

Guiding Those Left Behind In Arizona

CONTENTS

About The Book

We tried to make this book as comprehensive as possible so there are specialized sections of the book that do not apply to the general population and may not be of interest to you. The following GUIDE POSTS appear throughout the book. You can read the section if the situation applies to you or skip the section if it doesn't. Skipping the section will not affect the continuity of the book.

GUIDE POSTS

 The SPOUSE POST means that the information provided is specifically for the spouse of the decedent. If the decedent was single, you can skip this section.

 The CALL-A-LAWYER POST alerts you to a situation that may require the assistance of an attorney. See the end of this chapter for information about how to find a lawyer.

 The CAUTION POST alerts you to a potential problem. It is followed by a suggestion about how to avoid the problem.

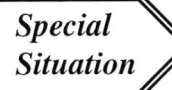 The SPECIAL SITUATION POST means that the information given in that paragraph applies to a particular event or situation; for example when the decedent dies a violent death. If the situation does not apply, you can skip the section.

The Organization of the Book

Guiding Those Left Behind refers to the things that need to be done in order to settle an Estate in Arizona. The purpose of this book is to guide the reader through that process. It explains:

1. How to tend to the funeral and burial
2. What agencies need to be notified
3. How to locate the decedent's property
4. What bills need (and do not need) to be paid
5. How to determine who is entitled to inherit the decedent's property
6. How to transfer the decedent's property to the proper beneficiary

We devoted a chapter to each of these 6 steps; and for those who are in charge of settling an Estate, we placed a CHECK LIST at the end of Chapter 6 summarizing those things that need to be done. Once you read Chapters 1 through 6 you will be able to identify those problems that can happen when someone dies. Using those Chapters as a base, you can set up your own Estate Plan so that your family is not burdened by similar problems. The rest of the book (Chapters 7, 8 and 9) suggests different methods you can use to accomplish this goal.

GLOSSARY

This book is designed for the average reader. Legal terminology has been kept to a minimum. There is a glossary at the end of the book in the event you come across a legal term that is not familiar to you.

FICTITIOUS NAMES AND EVENTS

The examples in this book are based loosely on actual events; however, all names are fictitious; and the events, as portrayed, are fictitious.

Reading the Law

Where applicable, we identified the state statute or federal statute that is the basis of the discussion. We did this as a reference, and also to encourage the general public to read the law as it is written. Prior to the Internet the only way you could look up the law was to physically take yourself to the local courthouse law library or the law section of a public library. Today, all of the state and federal statutes are literally at your finger tips. They are just a mouse click away on the Internet.

To look up the law all you need is the address of the Web site and the identifying number of the statute.

 FEDERAL STATUTES
http://www4.law.cornell.edu/uscode
ARIZONA STATUTES
http://www.azleg.state.az.us

Arizona has revised their statutes into 49 Titles. For example, Title 14 is Trusts, Estates & Protective Proceedings.

Each title is divided into numbered sections. We will refer to a statute by its Title number and the number of the Section. For example, (ARS 14-2102) refers to the Arizona Revised Statues Title 14, section 2102 of Title. To look up the statute, go to the Arizon Statute Web site and type 14-2102 in the search box.

If you come across a topic that you think is important, you may find it both interesting and profitable to actually read the law as written.

Paul B. Bartlett, Esq.

PAUL B. BARTLETT, ESQ. has been a member of the Arizona State Bar since 1976. He received his Bachelor of Arts degree with honors from the University of Wisconsin, Madison in 1972. He earned his Juris Doctor from Syracuse College of Law in 1975.

Paul Bartlett has been practicing in Tucson since 1976. He concentrates in the field of Elder Law (Trusts, Estates, Probate, Guardianhip, Medicaid Planning, and Conservatorships).

In 1983, while teaching an evening Hebrew course, two students came to class dejected. They had been informed that five of their relatives were diagnosed with Alzheimers's disease within the space of one month. The students subsequently formed a local chapter of the Alzheimer's Association and prevailed on Paul to volunteer his services. He soon found himself elected as President of the chapter. He remains as an active Board member.

Paul also has served as President of the Arizona State Chapter of the National Academy of Elder Law Attorneys. When he is not practicing law, Paul swims on a Masters Swim Team, concertizes with the guitar and sings in Arabic, Spanish, Hebrew, and Ladino.

For more information about Paul, visit his Website at: www.tucsonelderlaw.com.

THE DESIGN ARTIST

LUBOSH CECH designed the cover of this book. He is a renowned artist, with extensive educational background and professional work experience. He studied design, applied art, and painting in his native Prague, Czech Republic. He also studied in Italy at the University of Bologna. Since moving to the United States in 1984, Mr. Cech has been designing art exhibitions, working as an art director, and graphic designer. Mr. Cech is a photographer and often incorporates his photographs into his art work.

Lubosh Cech is the founder of OKO DESIGN STUDIO located in Portland, Oregon. He designs promotional materials for print and digital media. He has received numerous rewards for both graphic design and painting. For more information about Mr. Cech and the OKO Design Studio visit his Web site.
http://www.okodesignstudio.com

The cover photograph is by PhotoDisc. The name of the photo is *Rainbow In Grand Canyon*.

Amelia E. Pohl, Esq.

Before becoming an attorney in 1985, AMELIA E. POHL taught mathematics on both the high school and college level. During her tenure as Associate Professor of Mathematics at Prince George's Community College in Maryland, she wrote several books including

Probability: A Set Theory Approach
Principals of Counting
Common Stock Sense.

During her practice of law Attorney Pohl observed that many people want to reduce the high cost of legal fees by performing or assisting with their own legal transactions. Attorney Pohl found that, with a bit of guidance, people are able to perform many legal transactions for themselves. Attorney Pohl utilizes her background as teacher, author and attorney to provide that "bit of guidance" to the general public in the form of self-help legal books that she has written. Amelia E. Pohl is currently "translating" this book for the remaining 49 states:

Guiding Those Left Behind in Maine
Guiding Those Left Behind In North Dakota
Guiding Those Left Behind In Wyoming, etc.

ACKNOWLEDGMENT

When someone dies, the family attorney is often among the first to be called. Family members have questions about whether Probate is necessary, who to notify, how to get possession of the assets, etc. Over the years, as we practiced in the field of Elder Law, we noticed that the questions raised were much the same family to family. We agreed that a book answering such questions would be of service to the general public.

We also observed, that those who had experience in settling the Estate of a loved one were more understanding of the process, and better able to make decisions about how to arrange their own finances to avoid problems that could arise in settling an Estate. We named the book *Guiding Those Left Behind*. The "Guiding" refers to the guidance that this book gives in the event you need to settle the Estate of your loved one. It also refers to the guidance that you can give to your family by setting up your own Estate Plan so that your family is not burdened by unnecessary costs and delays in settling your Estate.

We wish to thank all of the clients, whom we have had the honor and pleasure to serve, for providing us with the impetus to produce this book.

When You Need A Lawyer

The purpose of the book is to give the reader a basic understanding of what needs to be done when someone dies in Arizona, and to provide information about how a person can arrange his own affairs to avoid problems for his own family. It is not intended as a substitute for legal counsel or any other kind of professional advice. If you have a legal question, you should seek the counsel of an attorney. When looking for an attorney, consider three things: EXPERTISE, COST and PERSONALITY.

EXPERTISE

The State Bar of Arizona has a certification program for eight areas of law BANKRUPTCY, CRIMINAL, ESTATE & TRUST, FAMILY LAW, INJURY AND WRONGFUL DEATH, REAL ESTATE, TAX, and WORKERS' COMPENSATION. To be certified by the Arizona Bar as a specialist in these areas, the attorney must have practiced in that area of law for at least two years and must pass a comprehensive Arizona Bar Certification Examination.

The State Bar of Arizona has a Lawyer Referral Service. You can call them at (602) 340-7300 and ask for a referral to an attorney in your county who is certified in the area of law that you seek. The Arizona Bar has a Web site that gives the name and telephone numbers of all of the Board Certified Attorneys in the state of Arizona.

 THE STATE BAR OF ARIZONA
http://azbar.org/FindingLawyer

Certification is just one of the criteria to consider. Many fine attorneys are experienced in an area of law, but have not taken the time, effort or expense to become certified in a given field.

One of the most reliable ways to find an attorney is through personal referral. Ask your friends, family or business acquaintances if they used an attorney for the field of law that you seek and whether they were pleased with the results. It is important to employ an attorney who is experienced in the area of law you seek. Your friend may have a wonderful Estate Planning attorney, but if you suffered an injury to your body, you need an attorney who is experienced in Personal Injury.

Before employing an attorney for a job, ask how long he has practiced that type of law and what percentage of his practice is devoted to that type of law.

COST

In addition to the attorney's experience, it is important that you check out what you can expect to pay in attorney's fees. When you call for an appointment ask what the attorney will charge for the initial consultation and the approximate cost for the service you seek. Ask whether there will be any additional costs such as filing fees, accounting fees, expert witness fees, etc.

If the least expensive attorney is out of your price range, there are two state agencies that provide legal assistance. The **ARIZONA MODEST MEANS PROJECT** offers legal assistance for those who cannot afford an attorney, but who make too much money to qualify for free legal services. They provide a free 30 minute initial consultation and a modest hourly rate thereafter. You reach them at **(602) 266-2322**.

For other agencies that offer counseling to persons with low income, you can look in the telephone book for the Legal Aid or Legal Service office nearest you or you can call (602) 252-4804 and they will refer you the office nearest you.

PERSONALITY

Of equal importance to the attorney's experience and legal fees, is your relationship with the attorney. How easy was it to reach the attorney? Did you go through layers of receptionists and legal assistants before being allowed to speak to the attorney? Did the attorney promptly return your call? If you had difficulty reaching the attorney, then you can expect similar problems should you employ that attorney.

Did the attorney treat you with respect? Did the attorney treat you paternally with a "father knows best" attitude or did he treat you as an intelligent person with the ability to understand the options available to you and the ability to make your own decision based on the information provided to you?

Are you able to understand and easily communicate with the attorney? Is he speaking to you in plain English or is his explanation of the matter so full of legalese to be almost meaningless to you?

Do you find the attorney's personality to be pleasant or grating? Sometimes people rub each other the wrong way. It is like rubbing a cat the wrong way. Stroking a cat from head to tail is pleasing to the cat, but petting it in the opposite direction, no matter how well intended, causes friction. If the lawyer makes you feel annoyed or uncomfortable, find another attorney.

It is worth the effort to take the time to interview as many attorneys as it takes to find one with the right expertise, fee schedule and personality for you.

The First Week

1

Dealing with the death of a close family member or friend is difficult. Not only do you need to deal with your own emotions, but often with those of your family and friends. Sometimes their sorrow is more painful to you than what you are experiencing yourself.

In addition to the emotional impact of a death, there are many things that need to be done, from arranging the funeral and burial, to closing out the business affairs of the *decedent* (the person who died) and finally giving whatever property is left to the proper beneficiary.

The funeral and burial take only a few days. Wrapping up the affairs of the decedent may take considerably longer. This chapter explains what things you (the spouse or closest family member) need to do during the first week, beginning at the moment of death and continuing through the funeral.

 MALE GENDER USED

Rather than use "he/she" or "his/her" for simplicity
(and hoping not to offend anyone)
we will refer to the decedent and his
Personal Representative using the male gender.

References to other people will be in both genders.

AUTOPSIES

In today's high tech world of medicine, doctors are fairly certain of the cause of death, but if there is a question as to the cause of death, the doctor may ask permission to perform an autopsy. If the decedent signed a HEALTH CARE POWER OF ATTORNEY authorizing an autopsy, the person he appointed as his HEALTH CARE AGENT can give permission for the procedure (ARS 36-3224). If the decedent did not authorize an autopsy, consent may be given by the person taking responsibility for the burial: parent, surviving spouse, child, Guardian, next of kin. If none of these are available, a friend, or whoever has legal responsibility for the burial may give permission (ARS 36-832).

The person who authorizes the autopsy must agree to pay for it because the cost of the examination is not covered under most health insurance plans. And that cost could be sizeable, running anywhere from several hundred to several thousand dollars, but it may be in the family's best interest to consent to the autopsy. The examination might reveal a genetic disorder that could be treated if it later appears in another family member. Death from a car "accident" could have been a heart attack at the wheel. Perhaps the patient who died suddenly in a hospital was misdiagnosed. The nursing home resident could have died from negligence and not old age. Even if none of these are found, knowing the cause of death with certainty is better than not knowing.

That was the case with the family of an elderly woman who was taken to the hospital complaining of stomach pains. The doctors thought she might be suffering from gallbladder disease but she died before they could effectively treat her.

A doctor suggested that an autopsy be performed to determine the actual cause of death. The woman had three daughters, one of whom objected to the autopsy: "Why spend that kind of money? It won't bring Mom back."

The daughter's wishes were respected, however over the years as they aged and became ill with their own various ailments, they would undergo physical examinations. As part of taking their medical history, doctors routinely asked "And what was the cause of your mother's death?" None could answer the question.

This is not a dramatic story. No mysterious genetic disorder ever occurred in any of her daughters, nor in any of their children. But each daughter (including the one who objected) at some point in her life, was confronted with the nagging question "What did Mom die of?"

AUTOPSIES PERFORMED BY THE MEDICAL EXAMINER

When a person dies, a physician must sign a medical certification stating the cause of death. This is not a problem if a person dies in a hospital or nursing home from natural causes. If he dies at home and the death was expected, the treating physician or nurse practitioner can be contacted to sign the medical certificate verifying that the decedent died of natural causes. But if a person dies, suddenly, at home and he was not under the care of a physician, whoever discovers the body must call 911 to summon the police. The peace officer will call the Coroner to determine the cause of death (ARS 11-593).

If the death occurred under questionable circumstances your family can ask the county Medical Examiner to conduct an autopsy (ARS 11-597). If the Medical Examiner thinks the examination is warranted, there will be no charge to the decedent's family or to his Estate. However, if the Medical Examiner thinks the test unnecessary, he can still have the autopsy performed, however whoever authorizes the procedure must agree to be responsible for payment.

The Medical Examiner will order an autopsy whenever any of the following exist:
- ⇨ a public health risk
- ⇨ evidence of a crime
- ⇨ evidence of inadequate health care
- ⇨ no clinically evident cause of death (ARS 11-593).

Once the Medical Examiner takes possession of a body, it will not be released until the examination is complete. In the interim, the family can proceed with arrangements for the funeral. The funeral director will contact the Coroner or Medical Examiner to determine when he can pick up the body and proceed with the funeral arrangements.

AUTOPSIES PERFORMED BY THE INSURANCE COMPANY

Under Arizona law, any company that issues a disability insurance policy has the right to include a provision in the policy giving the company authority to perform an autopsy on the deceased insured person (ARS 20-1354).

The cost of the autopsy must be paid for by the insurance company, so they will not order an autopsy unless there is some important reason to do so, such as whether the cause of death is covered under that policy.

ANATOMICAL GIFTS

Hospital personnel determine whether a mortally ill patient is a candidate for an organ donation. Early on in the donor program those over 65 were not considered as suitable candidates. Today, however, the condition of the organ, and not the age, is the determining factor.

The federal government has established regional Organ Procurement Organizations throughout the United States to coordinate the donor program. The Organ Procurement Organization for the state of Arizona is located in Phoenix. It is called the **DONOR NETWORK OF ARIZONA**. If it is decided that the patient is a candidate, the hospital will contact the Donor Network to determine whether the patient is a suitable donor.

GIFT AUTHORIZED PRIOR TO DEATH

If, before death, the decedent made an anatomical gift by signing a donor card, then hospital personnel or the donor's doctor need to be made aware of the gift in quick proximity to the time of death — preferably before death. If it is determined that the donation is medically acceptable, the gift will be made. No family member need give permission, provided the hospital has a copy of the decedent's unrevoked donor card (ARS 36-842).

GIFT AUTHORIZED BY THE FAMILY

If no donor card is on record, and it is determined that the decedent is a suitable donor, someone who is specially trained will approach the family to request permission for the donation.

Arizona statute 36-843 establishes an order of priority to authorize the donation:

1st The Agent appointed in the decedent's Health Care Power of Attorney

2nd The decedent's court appointed Guardian (if any)

3rd The spouse, unless legally separated

4th A majority of the decedent's adult children

5th A parent of the decedent

6th If unmarried, the decedent's domestic partner, if no one else has assumed financial responsibility for the patient.

7th adult brother or sister

8th a close friend

If permission is obtained from a family member and there are others in the same or a higher priority, then an effort must be made to contact those people and ask their permission. For example, if the brother of the decedent agrees to the gift (7th in priority) and an adult child is reasonably available for consultation (4th in priority), then the child needs to be made aware of the gift. No donation may be made if a member of a prior class objects to the gift. Arizona law also prohibits an anatomical gift if the decedent ever expressed his opposition to such donation (ARS 36-846).

AFTER THE DONATION

Once the donation is made the body is delivered to the funeral home and prepared for burial or cremation as directed by the family. The donation does not disfigure the body so there can be an open casket viewing if the family so wishes.

The Donor Network will keep in touch with the donor's family. They will provide the family with basic demographic information about the donation, such as the age, sex, marital status, number of children and occupation of the recipient of the gift. If the donor's family wishes, the Donor Network will provide them with updates during the year following the donation.

If the recipient of the gift wishes to write to the donor's family to thank them for the gift, the Donor Network will contact the donor's family and ask if they wish to receive the letter. If not, then the letter is kept on file in the event that the donor's family may want to read it at a later date.

GIFT FOR EDUCATION OR RESEARCH

Consider offering to release the body for the purpose of education or research in the event the decedent signed a donor card, but was not an appropriate candidate for an organ donation.

You can offer to release the body to the University of Arizona, Department of Cell Biology and Anatomy to be used for education or research:

University of Arizona
College of Medicine
Department of Cell Biology and Anatomy
1501 North Campbell Avenue
Tucson, AZ 85724-5044

They prefer advance registration, but will consider donations from the next of kin or the decedent's Health Care Agent. You will need to call the University's Department of Cell Biology and Anatomy at (520) 626-1801 within 24 hours after the death to determine whether they will accept the body.

The University will not accept bodies from those who have died from a contagious disease or from crushing injuries or who are extremely obese. They currently charge a transportation fee. You should ask what will be charged when you call to offer the donation.

The study can take up to two years to complete. At the end of the study the remains are cremated. The *cremains* (cremated remains) will be placed in a cemetery that is local to the university; or if the family wishes, the cremains will be delivered to the next of kin.

CAVEAT: Federal law prohibits payment for organ donations (42 U.S.C. 274 e). There is no ban on payments made to prepare organs or tissue for transplantation, nor is there any ban on charges made to transport bodies or body parts. Not-for-profit, as well as for-profit, companies have sprung up that are in the business of preparing and delivering body parts. These companies request donations from families — so they are not violating federal law by paying for the donation. The company prepares the body tissue or other parts of the donated body, and then distributes the parts throughout the United States to physicians, hospitals, research centers, etc. In many cases the monies charged for preparation and transportation includes a sizable profit.

If a company or organization other than the Donor Network of Arizona approaches you to make a donation, before agreeing, you may want to learn about the company that is making the request.

> *What is the name of the company?*
> *Where are their main headquarters located?*
> *What is their primary business activity?*
> *What is the name and job description of the*
> *person making the request?*

DETERMINE THE END USE OF THE DONATION

You may want to ask what they intend to do with the tissue or body part. If it is being used for research, then what type of research? Where is the research being conducted? If it will be used for transplantation, what agency (doctor, hospital) will receive the donation and where is that agency located?

Once you have this information you can make an informed decision as to whether you wish to make the donation to that organization.

THE FUNERAL

Approximately ten percent of deaths occur suddenly because of accident, suicide, foul play or undetected illness. But, in general, death occurs after a lengthy illness, with a common scenario being that of an aged person who dies after being ill for several months, if not years. In such case, family and friends are prepared for the happening. Expected or not, the first job is the disposition of the body.

THE PREARRANGED FUNERAL

Increasingly, people are arranging, in advance, for their own funeral and burial. This makes it easier on the family both financially and emotionally. All the decisions have been made and there is no guessing what the decedent would have wanted.

If the decedent made provision for his burial, you should come across a cemetery deed or perhaps a certificate for a burial plot. If he made provision for his funeral, you should find a PREARRANGEMENT FUNERAL PLAN. You need to read the contract to determine what provisions were made. If the Plan was paid by installments, you need to determine whether it is paid in full. You also need to find out whether the contract was a fixed price agreement or whether there will be additional charges.

If you cannot locate the contract, but you know the decedent made provision for his burial and funeral, call the funeral home and ask them to send you a copy of the contract. If you believe the decedent purchased a Prearrangement Funeral Agreement but you do not know the name of the funeral home, call the local funeral homes. Many local funeral homes are owned by national firms with computer capacity to identify people who have purchased a contract at any of their many locations.

Once you have possession of the Agreement, take it with you to the funeral home and go over the terms of the Agreement with the funeral director. Inquire whether there will be any charge that is not included in the contract.

MAKING FUNERAL ARRANGEMENTS

If the decedent died unexpectedly or without having made any prior funeral arrangements then your first job is to choose a funeral director and make arrangements for the funeral or cremation. Most people choose the nearest or most conveniently located funeral home without comparison shopping. However prices for these services can vary significantly. Savings can be had if you take the time to make a few phone calls.

Receiving price quotes by telephone is your right under both Arizona and federal law. Federal Trade Commission ("FTC") Rule 453.2(b)(1) and Arizona statute 32-1375 require a funeral director to give an accurate telephone quote of the prices of his goods and services. Funeral homes are listed in the telephone directory under FUNERAL DIRECTORS. If you live in a small town, there may be only one or two listings. If such is the case, check out funeral homes in the next largest city.

Funeral directors usually provide the following services:
➢ arrange for the transportation of the body
  to the funeral home and then to the burial site
➢ obtain a disposition-transit permit
➢ arrange for the embalming or cremation of the body
➢ arrange funeral and memorial services
  and the viewing of the body
➢ obtain information for the death certificate
➢ order copies of the death certificate for the family
➢ have memorial cards printed.

To compare prices you will need to determine:

✧ what is included in the price of a basic funeral plan

✧ whether you can expect any additional cost.

It may be necessary to have the body embalmed if you are going to have a viewing. Embalming is not necessary if you order a direct cremation or an immediate burial without a viewing. Federal Trade Commission Rule 453.5 prohibits the funeral home from charging an embalming fee unless you order the service.

If the decedent did not own a burial space, then that cost must be included when making funeral arrangements.

PURCHASING THE CASKET

When comparison-shopping, you will find that the single most expensive item in the funeral arrangement is the casket. Most funeral directors will quote you a price for a basic funeral plan that does not include the cost of the casket. Directors usually quote a range of prices for the casket, saying that you will need to come in and choose the casket at the time you contract for the funeral.

When selecting a casket you need to be aware that there may be a considerable mark-up in the price quoted by the funeral director. You do not need to go "sole source" when purchasing the casket. You can purchase the casket elsewhere and have it delivered to the funeral home to be used instead of the one offered by the funeral director. Funeral homes are required to accept caskets purchased elsewhere, and they may not charge a handling fee for accepting that casket. But if the price list given to you by the funeral home states that the price of their casket includes a specific dollar amount for basic services, then the funeral director is allowed to add that dollar amount to the charge for his services, should you purchase the casket elsewhere (FTC Rule 453.2, 453.4).

Caskets are not usually displayed for sale in a shopping mall, so most of us have no idea of the going price for a casket. With the advent of the Internet, you can learn all about the cost of any item, even a casket, by using your search engine to find a retail casket sales dealer. If you are not computer literate, you can locate the nearest retail casket sales outlet by looking in the yellow pages under CASKETS. You may need to look in the telephone directory for the nearest large city to find a listing. By making a call to a retail casket sales dealer, you will become knowledgeable in the price range of caskets. You can then decide what is a reasonable price for the product you seek.

The best time to do your comparison shopping is before you go to the funeral home to arrange for the funeral. Once you have determined what you should pay for the casket, it is only fair to give the funeral director the opportunity to meet that price. If you cannot reach a meeting of the minds, then you can always order the casket from the retail sales dealer and have it delivered to the funeral home.

ON-LINE FUNERAL SERVICES

The Internet is changing the way the world does business, and the funeral industry is no exception. A growing number of mortuaries are offering live Webcasts of funerals and wakes for those who are unable to pay their respects in person.

There are Websites where you can post an obituary. There are on-line memorial chat rooms as well as on-line eulogies and testimonials. There is even a Website that offers a posthumous e-mail service which allows people to leave final messages for friends and relatives. You can locate these services using your favorite search engine and typing in "obituaries."

THE CREMATION

Increasingly people are opting for cremation. THE CREMATION ASSOCIATION OF NORTH AMERICA reports that more than 57% of those who die in Arizona each year are cremated. That percentage is growing. The reasons for choosing cremation are varied, but for the majority, it is a matter of finances. The cost of cremation is approximately one-sixth that of an ordinary funeral and burial. A major saving is the cost of the casket. No casket is necessary for the cremation and Federal law prohibits a funeral director from saying that a casket is required for a direct cremation (FTC Rule 453.3 (b)ii). You may need a suitable container to deliver the body to the crematory. After the cremation, you will need an urn for the ashes.

If you are having a memorial service in a place of worship and no viewing of the body before the cremation, consider contracting with a facility that does cremations only. Look in the telephone book under CREMATION SERVICES. You will also see cremation "societies" in the telephone book. Some are for-profit and others not-for-profit. You can also find advertisements for cremation services on the Internet.

Under Arizona law, the funeral director must obtain authorization before he can embalm or cremate the decedent. Arizona law gives an order of priority for those who have the right to authorize the procedure:
1st the surviving spouse   2nd a surviving adult child
3rd a surviving parent   4th an adult brother or sister
5th the Executor of the decedent's Estate
6th the Guardian of the decedent at the time of death
7th the person designated by the county to handle
      the funeral arrangements (ARS 32-1365.02).

THE OVERWEIGHT DECEDENT

If the decedent weighs more than 300 pounds, you need to check to see if the Cremation service has facilities large enough to handle the body. If you cannot locate a crematory that can accommodate the body, you will need to make burial arrangements.

THE DECEDENT WITH A PACEMAKER

Cremating a body with a pacemaker or any radiation producing device can cause damage to the cremation chamber or to the person performing the cremation. If the decedent was wearing such electronic aid, it needs to be removed prior to the cremation. Some veterinary hospitals are implanting used pacemakers into pets who are suffering from heart disease. If the decedent was an animal advocate, consider making a donation of the pacemaker to the hospital in his memory.

DISPOSING OF THE CREMAINS

If the cremains are to be placed in a cemetery, you need to obtain a suitable urn for the burial. The container provided by the crematory can be used, or you can purchase the urn from the funeral director or crematory service director. Urns cost much less than caskets, but they can cost several hundred dollars. You may wish to do some comparison shopping by calling a retail sales casket dealer.

Many cemeteries have a separate section or building called a *columbarium*, which is especially designed to store urns. Some cemeteries allow the cremains of a family member to be placed in an occupied family plot or mausoleum. If you wish to have the cremains placed in an occupied mausoleum or family plot, you need to call the cemetery and ask them to explain their policy as it relates to the burial of urns in an occupied site.

If the decedent is to be buried in another state, you will need to make arrangements for the transporation of the body.Many states, including Arizona, require a Disposition-Transit Permit for burial or removal from the state where the death occurred (ARS 36-326). If services are to be held in Arizona and in another state, contact a local funeral director and he will make arrangements with the out-of-state funeral home for the transportation of the body.

If you do not plan to have services conducted in Arizona, you can contact the out-of-state funeral director and ask them to effect the transfer. Many funeral homes belong to a national network of funeral homes, so both the local and the out-of-state funeral director usually have the means to make arrangements to transport the body.

TRANSPORTING CREMAINS

If the body has been cremated, you can transport the cremains yourself, either by carrying the ashes as part of your carry-on luggage or by arranging with the airline to transport the ashes as cargo. Have a certified copy of the death certificate and the Disposition-Transit Permit ready in the event that you need to identify the cremains of the decedent.

In these days of heightened security, it is important to call the airline before departure and ask whether they have any special regulation or procedure regarding the transportation of human ashes.

SPOUSE | THE MILITARY BURIAL

Subject to availability of burial spaces, an honorably discharged veteran and his dependent child and his unremarried spouse may be buried in a national military cemetery. Some cemeteries are closed to new internments, however, they may have room for cremated remains or for the casketed remains of a family member of someone currently buried in that cemetery.

There are two national cemeteries in Arizona.
The Prescott National Cemetery does not have any more burial plots available, however, in 2006 they plan to build a columbarium to house the cremated remains of Veterans. Burial spaces are available at:

National Memorial Cemetery Of Arizona
23029 North Cave Creek Road
Phoenix, AZ 85024
Telephone: (480) 513-3600

In addition, there is the state Veteran's Cemetery:

Southern Arizona Veteran's Memorial Cemetery
1300 Buffalo Soldier Trail
Sierra Vista, AZ 85635
Telephone: (520) 458-7144

ARLINGTON NATIONAL CEMETERY
An honorably discharged veteran can be buried in the national military cemetery at Arlington, Virginia. The Department of the Army is in charge of the Arlington National Cemetery. You can call the Interment Service Branch at (703) 607-8585 for information about having a veteran buried there.

THE COST OF A
MILITARY BURIAL

Burial space in a National Cemetery is free of charge. Cemetery employees will open and close the grave and mark it with a headstone or grave marker without cost to the family. If requested, the local Veteran's Administration ("VA") will provide the family with a memorial flag. The VA will not pay to have the body transported to the cemetery, so the family needs to make arrangements with a funeral firm to transport the remains to the cemetery.

Regardless of where an honorably discharged veteran is buried, allowances may be available for the plot, and the burial and grave marker expenses. The amount varies depending on factors such as whether the veteran died because of a service related injury. The VA will not reimburse any burial or funeral expense for the spouse of a veteran. For information about re-imbursement of funeral and burial expenses you can call the VA at (800) 827-1000.

The Department of Veteran's Affairs has a Website with information on the following topics:

> National and Military Cemeteries
> Burial, Headstones and Markers
> State Cemetery Grants Program
> Obtaining Military Records
> Locating Veterans

 VA CEMETERY WEBSITE
http://www.cem.va.gov

BENEFITS FOR SPOUSE OF DECEASED VETERAN

SPOUSE

The surviving spouse of an honorably discharged veteran should contact the Veteran's Administration to determine whether he/she is eligible for any benefits. For example, if the decedent had minor or disabled children, his spouse may also be eligible for a monthly benefit of Dependency and Indemnity Compensation ("DIC").

Whether a surviving spouse is eligible for benefits depends on many factors including whether the decedent was serving on active duty, whether his death was service related, and the surviving spouse's assets and income. DIC benefits are discontinued should the surviving spouse remarry; however, the law allows payments to be resumed in the event that the subsequent marriage ends because of death or divorce.

For information about whether the surviving spouse is eligible for any benefit related to the decedent's military service call the VA at (800) 827-1000.

You can receive a printed statement of public policy: VA Pamphlet 051-000-00228-8 FEDERAL BENEFITS FOR VETERANS AND DEPENDENTS by sending a $7 check to:

THE SUPERINTENDENT OF DOCUMENTS
P.O. Box 371954
Pittsburgh, PA 15250-7954

Or you can download it without charge from the Internet.

 VETERAN'S ADMINISTRATION
http://www.va.gov

 **LAWYER** | THE WRONGFUL DEATH

It is important to have a Personal Injury attorney investigate any accidental death, to determine whether the death was caused by the wrongful act of a person, or company. If the accident was related to the decedent's job, the family may wish to consult with a Worker's Compensation attorney as well.

The decedent's surviving spouse, child, or parent have the right to be compensated for any economic loss, including lost financial support, they suffer because of a ***wrongful death*** (a death caused by a wrongful act). The person appointed by the Court to settle the decedent's Estate may sue on behalf of anyone who is entitled to be compensated for the loss. If there is no surviving spouse, child or parent, he can sue on behalf of the decedent's Estate.

The amount recovered will be distributed in proportion to loss suffered. If the decedent did not have a surviving parent, spouse or child, the money becomes part of his Estate to be distributed to the beneficiaries of the Estate (ARS 12-612).

A caregiver who abuses or neglects an incapacitated person can be found guilty of a Class 5 felony. If the decedent's death was caused by the abuse or neglect of his caregiver, then in addition to criminal penalties, the caregiver can be sued in civil court for damages suffered as a consequence of the abuse or neglect, as well as punitive damages, the costs to pursue the law suit, including attorney fees (ARS 46-455).

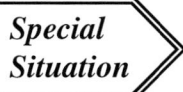 **VICTIMS OF CRIME COMPENSATION PROGRAM**

The State of Arizona reimburses crime victims and/or their families, who suffer loses that are not covered by insurance, public funds or any other compensation. If the decedent died because of a criminal act, you may be eligible for benefits under the **CRIME VICTIM COMPENSATION PROGRAM**. The program is administered by the **ARIZONA CRIMINAL JUSTICE COMMISSION (ARS 41-2407)**.

Compensation can be awarded for funeral and burial expenses (up to $5,000), for medical expenses, psychological counseling, lost support, lost wages, etc. Total compensation may not exceed $20,000.

To be eligible, all of the following must be true:

➢ The decedent was an innocent victim.
➢ The crime was reported to authorities within 72 hours of discovery of the crime.
➢ There was full cooperation with law enforcement officers by the victim and/or his family.
➢ Application for compensation was filed within two years from the commission of the crime or discovery of the body.

You can get a Crime Victim Compensation Program Application at the County Attorney's Office in the county where the crime occurred (ARS 13-4405). You can also download the application from the Criminal Justice Commission Website.

 ARIZONA CRIMINAL JUSTICE COMMISSION
http://acjc.state.az.us

Police make every effort to identify and locate the family of an unclaimed body. The county health officer or the Medical Examiner may authorize an anatomical gift, provided the decedent did not indicate an objection to the donation prior to his death (ARS 36-844).

BURYING THE INDIGENT

As explained on page 18, with the exception of transportation cost to the cemetery, an honorably discharged veteran can be buried without charge. If the decedent is identified as a member of a federally recognized Native American Tribe located within this state, the County Medical Examiner will notify the tribe of the death and give them the opportunity to take responsibility for the final disposition.

Under Arizona statute, the surviving spouse has the duty to make burial arrangements; and if no spouse, the duty falls to his adult children. If the decedent was a minor, his parents are responsible for the burial. If there is not enough money in the decedent's Estate to pay for the cost of the burial, and no family member can be found who is able to pay for the burial, the decedent will be cremated or given the normal county indigent burial. Payment for the cremation or burial will be made from the county treasury funds (ARS 11-600).

The family member who has the duty to pay for the funeral can be sued by whoever provided the service for two times the cost of the final disposition (ARS 36-831).

THE PROBLEM
FUNERAL OR BURIAL

The funeral and burial industry is well regulated by the state and federal government. Under Arizona law the following acts are subject to disciplinary action:

⊠ Delivering goods of a lesser quality than that presented to the purchaser as a sample

⊠ Using a false or misleading advertisement

⊠ Paying kick-backs to generate business (ARS 32-1301(54)).

Funeral directors are licensed professionals so it is unusual to have a problem with the funeral or burial or cremation. If, however, you had a bad experience with any aspect of the funeral, you can file a complaint with the state licensing agency.

State Board of Funeral Directors and Embalmers
1400 W. Washington, Room 230
Phoenix, AZ 85007
(602) 542-3095

This agency does not license cemeteries, so if your complaint has to do with the burial you can contact the state consumer protection agency of the Office of the Attorney General at (602) 542-3702 or you can call their toll free number (800) 352-8431.

 In addition to filing a complaint with the Board, you may wish to consult with an attorney who is experienced in litigation matters to learn of any other legal remedy that may be available to you.

Few things are more difficult to deal with than a missing person. The emotional turmoil created by the "not knowing" is often more difficult than the finality of death. The legal problems created by the disappearance are also more difficult than if the person simply died. It may take a two-part legal process — the appointment of a Conservator to handle the missing person's affairs in his absence, and a Probate procedure, if it is established that he is dead (ARS 14-3108).

APPOINTING A CONSERVATOR

An **Absentee** is a person who is missing and cannot be found after a diligent search. If the Absentee has business matters that need attending (bills that need to be paid, family to be supported), then his next of kin can ask the Probate Court to appoint a Conservator of the absentee's property (ARS 14-5401). The Conservator will manage the property, under court supervision, until the person can be found. You will need an attorney, experienced in Probate matters, to have the Conservator appointed.

BEGINNING THE PROBATE PROCEDURE

Anyone who has the right to inherit the Absentee's property can begin the Probate process any time there is sufficient evidence that the Absentee is dead, or after the Absentee has been missing for five years. The judge will hear evidence to determine whether the missing person should be presumed dead; and if so, the Probate proceeding can go forward. Should the Absentee show up at a later time, he will have the right to have his property restored to him (ARS 12-509).

THE DEATH CERTIFICATE

It is the job of the funeral director to provide information about the decedent to the State Registrar. The Office of Vital Records will prepare a death certificate based on that information. It is important that the information you give to the funeral or cremation director is correct. You need to check the form completed by the funeral director to be sure names are correctly spelled and dates correctly written. Once the information is sent to Vital Records, it will be difficult and time consuming to make a correction.

The funeral director will order as many certified copies of the death certificate as you request. Most establishments require an original certified copy and not a photocopy so you need to order sufficient certified copies. The following is a list of institutions that may request a certified copy:

✳ Each insurance company that insured the decedent or his property (health insurance, life insurance, car insurance, etc.)

✳ Each financial institution in which the decedent had money invested (brokerage houses, banks)

✳ The decedent's pension fund

✳ Each credit card company used by the decedent

✳ The IRS

✳ The Social Security Administration

✳ The Motor Vehicle Office

Some airlines and car rental companies offer a discount for short notice, emergency trips. If you have family flying in for the funeral, you may wish to order a few extra copies of the death certificate so that they may be able to obtain an airline or car rental discount.

Under Arizona law, death certificates are confidential records, so they restrict access to certified copies of the death certificate to just the following people:

⇨ the surviving spouse, or adult member of the decedent's immediate family (parent, sibling, adult child) or someone who is authorized in writing, by the family member.

⇨ an attorney or funeral director acting for the spouse or the immediate family

⇨ a governmental agency needing proof of death for medical, scientific or official purposes

⇨ an insurance company, bank or hospital which requires a certified copy of the death certificate for business purposes

⇨ a relative engaged in research for genealogical purposes (ARS 36-324).

If you wish to order certified copies of the death certificate at a later date, you can call the funeral director and ask him to do so, or if you are a qualified member of the decedent's family you can write to:

Office of Vital Records
P.O. Box 3887
Phoenix, AZ 85030

You should first call to determine the cost and what information they require to prove that you are entitled to receive a certified copy of the death certificate.

In state, call toll free (888) 816-5907

Out of state call (602) 364-1300.

WALK-IN

You can apply, in person, for a certified copy of the death certificate at   The Office of Vital Records

1818 West Adams Avenue

Phoenix, AZ   85007

During the first 30 days following the death, you can also obtain a certified copy from the county in which the death occurred. You can find the location of Vital Records Offices and information about what you will need in order to obtain a copy of the death certificate from the Office of Vital Records section of the Arizona Department of Health Services Website.

 ARIZONA DEPARTMENT OF HEALTH SERVICES

http://www.azdhs.gov

About Probate

Once a person dies, all of the property he owns as of the date of his death is referred to as the **decedent's Estate.** If the decedent owned property that was in his name only (not jointly or in trust for someone), some sort of court procedure may be necessary to determine who is entitled to ownership of the property. The name of the court procedure is **Probate**. In Arizons, Probate is conducted in the Superior Court (ARS 14-3201). We will use the term Court" or "Probate Court" to refer to the judge who is presiding over Probate matters.

The root of the word Probate is "to prove." It refers to the first job of the Probate Court, that is, to examine proof of whether the decedent left a valid Will. The second job of the Probate Court is to appoint someone to wrap up the affairs of the decedent by paying the cost of the Probate procedure, any outstanding bills, and then distributing whatever is left to the proper beneficiary.

If the decedent left a valid Will naming someone as *Executor* of his Estate, the Court will appoint that person for the job and issue *Letters Testamentary* giving him authority to administer the Estate. If the decedent died without a Will, the Probate Court will appoint someone to be the *Administrator* of his Estate and issue *Letters of Administration.* For simplicity we will refer to the person appointed by the Court to settle the decedent's Estate as the **Personal Representative**, and the document authorizing him to act, as **Letters**.

There are different ways to conduct a Probate procedure depending on the value of the property that is being Probated, and whether the decedent owned real property at the time of his death. We will refer to the property that is distributed as part of a Probate proceeding as the decedent's **Probate Estate** and the method of conducting the Probate as the **Estate Administration**.

Chapter 6 explains the different kinds of Estate Administration that are available in the state of Arizona.

But we are getting ahead of ourselves. First we need to determine whether a Probate procedure is necessary. To answer that question we need to know exactly what the decedent owned, so the next two chapters explain how to identify, and then locate, the decedent's assets.

Giving Notice Of The Death 2

Those closest to the decedent usually notify family members and close friends by telephone. The funeral director will arrange to have an obituary published in as many different newspapers as the family requests, but there is still the job of notifying the government and people who were doing business with the decedent. That job is the duty of whoever is appointed as Personal Representative of the decedent's Estate.

Arizona law gives an order of priority for the appointment of Personal Representative. Whoever the decedent named as Executor or Personal Representative in his Will has top priority. Once appointed, it is his job to give notice of the death. If the decedent died *intestate*, i.e. without a valid Will, the decedent's spouse has priority to be appointed as Personal Representative (ARS14-3203). If there is no spouse, the job falls to his next of kin. By *next of kin,* we mean those people who inherit the decedent's property according to Arizona's LAWS OF INTESTATE SUCCESSION. Those laws are explained in Chapter 5.

The person who has the job of settling the decedent's Estate should begin to give notice as soon as is practicable after the death. Two government agencies that need to be notified are the Social Security Administration and the IRS. This chapter gives their telephone number as well as other agencies that need to be notified.

NOTIFYING SOCIAL SECURITY

Many funeral directors will, as part of their service package, notify the Social Security Administration of the death. You may wish to check to see that this has been done. You can do so by calling (800) 772-1213. If you are hearing impaired call (800) 325-0778 TTY. You will need to give the Social Security Administration the full legal name of the decedent as well as his Social Security number and date of birth.

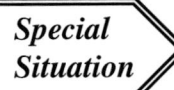 **Special Situation**   DECEDENT RECEIVING SOCIAL SECURITY

If the decedent was receiving checks from Social Security, you need to determine whether his last check needs to be returned to the Social Security Administration. Each Social Security check is a payment for the prior month, provided that person lives for the entire prior month. If the decedent died on the last day of the month, you should not cash the check for that month.

For example, if he died on July 31st, you need to return the check that the Social Security mailed out in August. If however, he died on August 1st the check sent in August need not be returned because that check was payment for the month of July.

If the Social Security check is electronically deposited into a bank account, notify the bank and the Social Security Administration that the account holder died. If the check needs to be returned, the Social Security Administration will withdraw it electronically from the bank account. You will need to keep the account open until the funds are withdrawn.

SPOUSE/CHILD'S SOCIAL SECURITY BENEFITS

SPOUSE

If the decedent had sufficient work credits, the Social Security Administration will give the decedent's widow(er) or if unmarried, then the decedent's minor children, a one-time death benefit in the amount of $255.

SURVIVORS BENEFITS:

The spouse (or former spouse) of the decedent may be eligible for Survivors Benefits. Benefits vary depending on the amount of work credits earned by the decedent; whether the decedent had minor or disabled children; the spouse's age; how long they were married; etc. The minor child of the decedent may be eligible for benefits regardless of whether the child's father (the decedent) ever married the child's mother. Paternity can be established by any one of several methods including the father acknowledging his child in writing or verbally to members of his family. For more information call the Social Security Administration at (800) 772-1213.

SOCIAL SECURITY BENEFITS

A spouse or former spouse can collect Social Security benefits based on the decedent's work record. This value may be greater than the spouse now receives. It is important to make an appointment with your local Social Security office and determine whether you as the spouse (or former spouse) or parent of decedent's minor child are eligible for any Social Security or Survivor benefit. You can down load publications that explain survivors benefits from the Internet.

 SOCIAL SECURITY ADMINISTRATION
http://www.ssa.gov

DECEDENT WITH GOVERNMENT PENSION

Any pension or annuity check received after the date of death of a federal retiree, or a survivor annuitant, needs to be returned to the U.S. Treasury. If the check is direct deposited to a bank account, call the financial institution and ask them to return the check. If the check is sent by mail, you need to return it to the return mail address on the Department of Treasury envelope in which the check was mailed. Include a letter explaining the reason for the return of the check and stating the decedent's date of death.

$$$ APPLY FOR BENEFITS $$$

A survivor annuity may be available to a surviving spouse, and/or minor or disabled child. In some cases, a former spouse may be eligible for benefits. Even though you notify the government of the death, they will not automatically give you benefits to which you may be entitled. You need to apply for those benefits by notifying the Office of Personnel Management ("OPM") of the death and requesting that they send you an application for survivor benefits. You can call them at (888) 767-6738 or you can write to:

U. S. OFFICE OF PERSONNEL MANAGEMENT
RETIREMENT OPERATIONS CENTER
Post Office Box 45
Boyers, PA 16017-4500

You will find brochures and information about Survivor's Benefits at the OPM Website.

 U.S. OFFICE OF PERSONNEL MANAGEMENT
http://www.opm.gov

Special Situation	DECEDENT WITH COMPANY PENSION OR ANNUITY

In most cases, pension and annuity checks are payment for the prior month. If the decedent received his pension or annuity check before his death, then no monies need be returned. Pension checks and/or annuity checks received after the date of death may need to be returned to the company. You need to notify the company of the death to determine the status of the last check sent to the decedent.

Before notifying the company, locate the policy or pension statement that is the basis of the income. That document should tell whether there is a beneficiary of the pension or annuity funds now that the pensioner or annuitant is dead. If you cannot locate the document, use the return address on the check envelope and ask the company to send you a copy of the plan. Also request that they forward to you any claim form that may be required in order for the survivor or beneficiary to receive benefits under that pension plan or policy.

If the pension/annuity check is direct deposited to the decedent's account, ask the bank to assist you in locating the company and notifying the company of the death.

DECEDENT WITH AN IRA or
QUALIFIED RETIREMENT PLAN ("QRP")

Anyone who is a beneficiary of an Individual Retirement Account ("IRA") or QRP needs to keep in mind that income taxes may not have been paid on monies placed in an IRA or QRP account. In such case, significant taxes may be due when the money is withdrawn. You need to learn what options are available to you as a beneficiary of the plan and the tax consequences of each option. You will need to ask an accountant how much will be due in taxes for each option. Once you know all the facts, you will be able to make the best choice for your circumstance.

SPOUSE There are special options available if the spouse is the beneficiary of the decedent's IRA account. The spouse has the right to withdraw the money from the account or roll it over into the spouse's own retirement account. Although the employer can explain options that are available, the spouse still needs to understand the tax consequence of making a particular choice. It is important to consult with an accountant or an attorney to determine the best way to go. There are time limits for exercising these options, so the spouse needs to investigate the matter as soon as is practicable.

If the decedent had a QRP, the plan may permit the spouse to roll the balance of the account into a new IRA. The spouse needs to contact the decedent's employer for an explanation of the plan and all the options that are available at this time.

NOTIFYING IRS

THE FINAL INCOME TAX RETURN
The surviving spouse can file a final joint federal income tax return. If there is no surviving spouse, then it is the Personal Representative's job to file the final return. If Probate is not necessary, whoever takes possession of the decedent's property needs to file the final federal income tax return. A final Arizona income tax return must be filed as well if the decedent had an adjusted gross income of $5,500 ($11,000 if married) (ARS 43-301).

The decedent's final federal income tax return (IRS form 1040) needs to be filed by April 15th of the year following the year in which he died. The state income tax return is due at the same time (ARS 43-325). You can get information about filing the final return by calling Arizona Taxpayer Information & Assistance at (602) 255-3381. You can call (800) 352-4090 toll free from area code 520 and 928. You can download forms and get information from the Arizona Department of Revenue Website.

 ARIZONA DEPT. OF REVENUE
http://www.azdor.gov

You may want to keep the decedent's bank account open until you determine whether the decedent is entitled to an income tax refund. See Chapter 6 for an explanation of how to obtain a tax refund.

THE GOOD NEWS
Monies inherited from the decedent are generally not counted as income to you, so you do not pay federal income tax on those monies. If the monies you inherit later earn interest or income for you, then of course you will report that income as you do any other type of income.

Both the federal and state government have the right to impose an *Estate Tax* on property transferred to a beneficiary as a result of the death. All the property owned as of the date of death becomes the decedent's *Taxable Estate.* This includes *real property* (residential lots, condominiums etc.) and *personal property* (life insurance policies, cars, business interests, securities, IRA accounts, etc.). It includes property held in the decedent's name alone, as well as property that he held jointly or in Trust. It also includes gifts given by the decedent during his lifetime that exceeded $10,000 per person, per year. In the year 2002, the *Annual Gift Tax Exclusion* was adjusted for inflation to $11,000 (26 U.S.C 2503). For most of us, this is not a concern because no federal Estate Tax need be paid unless the decedent's Taxable Estate exceeds the federal *Estate Tax Exclusion* amount. That value is currently two million dollars and is scheduled to go even higher:

YEAR	ESTATE TAX EXCLUSION AMOUNT
2006-2008	$2,000,000
2009	$3,500,000

Under current law, the federal Estate Tax is scheduled to be phased out in the year 2010, but reinstated once again in the year 2011 with an Exclusion Amount of $1,000,000 — unless lawmakers change the tax law once again.

There is an unlimited marital tax deduction for property transferred to the surviving spouse who is a U.S. citizen; so in most cases, no Estate tax need be paid if the decedent was married. Regardless of whether taxes are due, federal and state Estate tax returns must be filed whenever the decedent's Estate exceeds the federal Estate Tax Exclusion Amount in effect as of his date of death. Both state and federal return are due within nine months of the date of death (ARS 42-4004).

THE ARIZONA "PICK-UP" TAX

The Arizona Estate tax is based on the federal Estate Tax. The federal government imposes a tax on all property transferred because of the death. The federal government then grants an Estate Tax credit, so that no tax need be paid unless the amount transferred is more than a given dollar value. That dollar value is the federal Estate Tax Exclusion Amount (see prior page). The Arizona Estate tax is called a "pick-up" tax, because the state collects the tax that would have gone to the federal government had it not been for the federal Estate Tax Exclusion.

As with the federal Estate Tax, no tax need be paid to the state of Arizona, unless the decedent's Taxable Estate exceeds the current federal Tax Exclusion amount. However for those Estates that are larger than the Exclusion Amount, Estate Taxes will need to be paid to the federal government and to the state of Arizona. And that includes property transferred within the state regardless of whether the decedent was a resident of the state (ARS 42-4051).

As explained, the federal Estate Tax is scheduled to be phased out and then reinstated in 2011. The Arizona Estate Tax is based on the federal Estate Tax Exclusion Amount, so unless the legislature changes things, the Arizona Estate Tax will go the way of the federal Estate Tax.

Both state and federal government do not tax property passing to the decedent's spouse, however, once the surviving spouse dies, all of his Estate is subject to Estate taxes. As we will see in Chapter 7, setting up a Revocable Living Trust can significantly reduce the amount of federal and Arizona Estate Taxes that may need to be paid once the surviving spouse dies.

THE UN-UNIFIED GIFT TAX

As explained, in the year 2002, the federal Annual Gift Tax Exclusion was adjusted for inflation and increased from $10,000 to $11,000. It was increased again in 2006 to $12,000. The IRS keeps a running count of amounts you give to someone that exceed the Annual Gift Tax Exclusion that is effective in the year of the donation.

Although you are required to report amounts over theAnnual Exclusion value, no tax is due unless that running total is more than the federal lifetime Gift Tax Exclusion amount which is currently one million dollars. If your running total does not exceed that amount during your lifetime, once you die, the cumulative value of gifts reported to the IRS will be added to your Taxable Estate.

Up until the change in the tax law in 2001, the Gift and Estate Tax were unified. No Gift Tax needed to be paid unless the total value of the taxable gifts exceeded the federal Estate Tax Exclusion amount. That changed in 2004. In 2004, the federal Estate Tax Exclusion amount went up to $1,500,000, but the amount for the Gift Tax Exclusion remained at $1,000,000, so they are no longer unified.

To summarize:
If you make a gift to someone that is greater than the Annual Gift Tax Exclusion for that year, you must report the gift to the IRS. The IRS will keep count of values that you gave in excess of the Annual Gift Tax Exclusion. In 2004, and thereafter, if that sum exceeds $1,000,000, you will pay a Gift Tax on any amount you give that is over the Annual Gift Tax Exclusion. The Estate Tax is scheduled to be repealed in 2010, but not the Gift Tax.

Arizona does not have a Gift Tax at this time.

The current federal Estate tax is scheduled to be phased out in the year 2010, but a new Capital Gains Tax is scheduled for 2010 that may prove even more costly than the Estate Tax. The new Capital Gains Tax is related to the way inherited property is evaluated by the federal government. Real and personal property is inherited at a "stepped-up" basis, meaning that if the decedent's property increased in value from the time he acquired it, the beneficiary inherits the property at its fair market value as of the decedent's date of death.

For example, if the decedent bought stock for $20,000 and it is worth $50,000 as of his date of death, the beneficiary will take a step-up in basis of $30,000; i.e. the beneficiary inherits the stock at the current $50,000 value. If the beneficiary sells the stock for $50,000, he pays no Capital Gains Tax. If the beneficiary holds onto the stock and later sells it for $60,000, the beneficiary will pay a Capital Gains Tax only on the $10,000 increase in value since the decedent's death.

Up to 2009, there is no limit to the amount a beneficiary can take as a step-up in basis. But in 2010 caps are set in place. The decedent's Estate will be allowed a 1.3 million dollar step-up in basis, plus another 3 million for property passing to the surviving spouse (26 U.S.C. 1022(b)).

The new law could result in significant Capital Gains Taxes that the beneficiary must pay. For example, suppose in 2010 you inherit a business from your father that he purchased for $100,000 and it is now worth 2 million dollars. There is a capital gain of 1.9 million dollars, but you are allowed a step-up in basis of only 1.3 million. If you sell it for two million dollars, $600,000 of your inheritance will be subject to a Capital Gains Tax.

SPOUSE ➤ SELLING THE HOME

In the tough "ole days" the IRS used to allow Capital Gains Tax Exclusion (up to $125,000) on the sale of one's *homestead* (the principal residence). A person had to be 55 or older to take advantage of the Exclusion, and it was a once-in-a-lifetime tax break. If a married couple sold their home and took the Tax Exclusion it was "used up" and no longer available to either partner.

In these, the good times, the IRS allows you to sell your home and up to $250,000 ($500,000 for a married couple) of the profit is free of the Capital Gains Tax. There is no limit to the number of times you can use the Exclusion, provided you own and live in the home at least two of the last five years prior to the sale (26 U.S.C. 121).

If, under the old law, the decedent and his spouse used their "once in a lifetime" Homestead Tax Exclusion, with this new law, the surviving spouse can sell the homestead and once again take advantage of the tax break.

There are certain *Homestead Tax Exemptions* available for those of low income and who are disabled (ARS 42-11111). If the decedent was receiving a Homestead Tax Exemption, the County Assessor must be notified of the transfer of the property to a new owner. The new owner may want to check with the County Assessor to see if he qualifies for his own Tax Exemption.

The surviving spouse may be eligible for a widow(ers) Tax Exemption. There are several criteria to determine whether the surviving spouse is eligible, including income requirements and whether a minor or disabled child lives in the home. Upon remarriage, the surviving spouse will no longer qualify for a Homestead Tax Exemption.

The surviving spouse will need to contact the County Assessor's office and request information about eligibility for the Tax Exemption. A homeowner needs to apply between the first Monday in January and March 1st, to receive a Tax Exemption for that year (ARS 42-11153).

You can call the Department of Revenue for information about property taxes at (602) 716-6843 or you can get information from their Website.
http://www.azdor.gov

╱ **Special Situation** ╱   DECEDENT WITH A TRUST

A decedent who was the **Settlor** (or *Grantor*) of a Trust, was probably managing the Trust as *Trustee* during his lifetime. The document that sets out the terms of the Trust (the **Trust Agreement**) should name a **Successor Trustee** to manage the Trust now that the Settlor is deceased. The Agreement may instruct the Successor Trustee to make certain gifts once the Settlor dies or the Trust document may direct the Successor Trustee to hold money in trust for a beneficiary of the Trust.

 **☎ LAWYER**   IF YOU ARE SUCCESSOR TRUSTEE

If you are the Successor Trustee, then in addition to following the terms of the Trust, you are required to obey the laws of the state relating to the administration of the Trust. For example, within 30 days you need to give written notice of your acceptance of your job as Successor Trustee, to each beneficiary who is entitled to receive an income from the Trust (ARS 14-7303). You should consult with an attorney experienced in Estate Planning to help you administer the Trust according to the law and without any liability to yourself.

IF YOU ARE BENEFICIARY of the Trust, you need to get a copy of the Trust to learn how it will be administered as it relates to your interest in the Trust. Arizona law requires the Successor Trustee to give you a copy of the Trust, provided you ask for a copy. Most Trust documents are written in "legalese," so you may want to employ your own attorney to review the Trust, and to explain your rights under the Trust.

People and companies who were doing business with the decedent need to be notified of his death. This includes utility companies, credit card companies, banks, brokerage firms and any company that insured the decedent.

NOTIFY CREDIT CARD COMPANIES

You need to notify the decedent's credit card companies of the death. If you can find the contract with the credit card company, check to see whether the decedent had credit card insurance. If the decedent had credit card insurance, then the balance of the account is now paid in full. If you cannot find the contract, contact the company and get a copy of the contract along with a statement of the balance due as of the date of death.

DESTROY DECEDENT'S CREDIT CARDS

You need to destroy all of the decedent's credit cards. If you hold a credit card jointly with the decedent, then it is important to waste no time in closing that account and opening another in your name only.

That's something Barbara knows from hard experience. She and Hank never married but they did live together for several years before he died from liver disease. Hank came from a well to do family so he had enough money to support himself and Barbara during his long illness. Hank put Barbara on all of his credit card accounts so that she could purchase things when he became too ill to go shopping with her. After the funeral, Barbara had a gathering of friends and family at their apartment. Barbara was so preoccupied with her loss that she never noticed that Hank's credit cards were missing until the bills started coming in.

Barbara did not know who ran up the bills on Hank's credit cards during the month following his death. It was obvious that Hank's signature had been forged — but who forged it? One credit card company suspected that it might have been Barbara herself to get out of paying the bill by saying that the card had been stolen.

Because the cards were held jointly, Barbara became liable to either pay the charges to the credit card or prove that she did not make the purchases. She was able to clear her credit record but it took several months and she had to employ an attorney to help her do so.

NOTIFY INSURANCE COMPANIES

Examine the decedent's financial records to determine the name and telephone number of all of the companies that insured the decedent or his property. This includes real property insurance, motor vehicle insurance, health insurance and life insurance.

MOTOR VEHICLE INSURANCE

Locate the insurance policy for any type of motor vehicle owed by the decedent (car, truck, boat, airplane) and notify the insurance company of the death. Determine how long insurance coverage continues after the death. Ask the insurance agent to explain what things are covered under the policy. Is the motor vehicle covered for all types of casualty (theft, accident, vandalism, etc.) or is coverage limited in some way?

If you can continue coverage, then determine when the next insurance payment is due. Hopefully, the car will be sold or transferred to a beneficiary before that date, but if not, you need to arrange for sufficient insurance coverage during the Probate procedure.

| Special Situation > | ACCIDENTAL DEATH |

If the decedent died as a result of an accident, then check for all possible sources of accident insurance coverage including his homeowner's policy. Some credit card companies provide accident insurance as part of their contract with their card holders. If the decedent died in an automobile accident, check to see whether he was covered by any type of travel insurance, such as rental car insurance. If he belonged to an automobile club, such as AAA, then check whether he had accident insurance as part of his club membership.

LIFE INSURANCE COMPANIES

If the decedent's life was insured, you need to locate the policy and notify the company of his death. Call each life insurance company and ask what they require in order to forward the insurance proceeds to the beneficiary. Most companies will ask you to send them the original policy and a certified copy of the death certificate. Send the original policy by certified mail or any of the overnight services that require a signed receipt for the package. Make a copy of the original policy for your records before mailing the original policy to the company.

BANK ACCOUNT LIFE INSURANCE

Many banks, credit unions, savings and loan associations provide life insurance at no cost to the primary owner of the account. While the amounts are generally small ($1,000 to $5,000), it is insurance that is often overlooked when settling the decedent's affairs. If you do not find a record of such policy, contact each financial institution to determine whether such insurance is provided by the company.

IF YOU CANNOT LOCATE THE POLICY

If you know that the decedent was insured, but you cannot locate the insurance policy, you can contact the company and request a copy of the policy. A tougher question is how to locate the policy if you do not know the name of the insurance company. The American Council of Life Insurers offers suggestions that you may find helpful at the Missing Policy Inquiry page of their Website.

 AMERICAN COUNCIL OF LIFE INSURERS
http://www.acli.com

IF YOU CANNOT LOCATE THE COMPANY

If you cannot locate the insurance company it may be doing business under another name or it may no longer be doing business in the state of Arizona. Each state has a branch of government that regulates insurance companies doing business in that state. If you are having difficulty locating the insurance company you can call the Department of Insurance in the state where the policy was purchased and ask for assistance in locating the company. In Arizona, you can call the Department of Insurance at (800) 235-2548.

EAGLE PUBLISHING COMPANY OF BOCA has the telephone number of the Department of Insurance for each state at the PUBLIC INFORMATION section of its Website.
http://www.eaglepublishing.com

WORK RELATED INSURANCE

If the decedent was employed, check his records for information about work related benefits. He may have survivor benefits from a company or group life insurance plan and/or a retirement plan. Also check with the employer about company benefits. If the decedent belonged to a union, ask the employer who you can contact to determine whether there are any union benefits.

The decedent may have belonged to a professional, fraternal or social organization such as the local Chamber of Commerce, a Veteran's organization, the Kiwanis, AARP, the Rotary Club, etc. If he belonged to any such organization check to see whether the organization provided any type of insurance coverage.

 **BUSINESS OWNED BY DECEDENT**

If the decedent owned his own company or was a partner in a company he may have purchased "key man" insurance. Key man insurance is a policy designed to protect the company should a valuable employee become disabled or die. Benefits are paid to the company to compensate the company for the loss of someone who is essential to the continuation of the business. Ultimately the policy benefits those who inherit the business.

If the decedent had an ownership interest in an ongoing business (sole proprietor, shareholder or partner) there may be a shareholder's or partnership agreement requiring the company to purchase the decedent's share of the business. The Personal Representative or his attorney needs to investigate to see if there was a key man insurance policy and/or such purchase agreement.

CORPORATE OWNER
OR STATUTORY AGENT

If the decedent was the sole owner and officer of a corporation , the ARIZONA CORPORATION COMMISSION needs to be notified of the change of ownership. There may need to be a Probate proceeding in order to transfer ownership of the company to the proper beneficiary, so it may take some time before new officers and directors are appointed.

Arizona statute requires each corporation to continuously maintain a *Statutory Agent* in this state. If the decedent was the Statutory Agent of the company, the Corporation Commission needs to be notified of the identity of the Statutory Agent as soon as is practicable (ARS 10-502). Forms to change officers and/or Statutory Agent can be obtained by writing to:
ARIZONA CORPORATION COMMISSION
400 W. Congress Suite 221
Tucson, AZ 85701
or you can download the form from the Internet.

 ARIZONA CORPORATION COMMISSION
http://www.cc.state.az.us

Arizona statute 10-502 allows changes to be made as part of the next annual report so if the change is not made sooner, it can be done at the same time the annual report is filed.

STATUS REPORT If you were not actively involved in running the business, you might want to call the Arizona Corporations Commission at (602) 542-3026 for information about the company (names, addresses of officers and directors, number of company shares, whether fees are current, etc.).

HOMEOWNER'S INSURANCE

If the decedent owned his own home, then check whether there is sufficient insurance coverage on the property. The decedent may have neglected to increase his insurance as the property appreciated in value. If you think the property may be vacant for some period of time, it is important to have vandalism coverage included in the policy. Once the property is sold, or transferred to the proper beneficiary, you can have the policy discontinued or transferred to the new owner. The decedent's Estate should receive a refund for the unused portion of the premium.

MORTGAGE INSURANCE

If the decedent had a mortgage on any parcel of real estate that he owned, he might have arranged with his lender for an insurance policy that pays off the mortgage balance in the event of his death. Look at the closing statement to see whether there was a charge for mortgage insurance. Also check with the lender to determine if such a policy was purchased.

If there was no mortgage insurance, and the decedent was the sole owner, the beneficiary of the property needs to make arrangements with the lender to continue making payments on the mortgage or to refinance the loan.

NOTIFY THE HOMEOWNER'S ASSOCIATION

If the decedent owned a condominium or a residence regulated by a homeowner's association, the association will need to be notified of the change of ownership. Once the property is transferred, the new owner will need to contact the association to learn of the rules and regulations of the association. The new owner will need to arrange to have notices of dues and assessments forwarded to him.

HEALTH INSURANCE

The health insurance carrier probably knows of the death, but it is a good idea to contact them to determine what coverage the decedent had under that insurance plan. If you cannot find the original policy, have the insurance company send you a copy of the policy so that you can determine whether medical treatment given to the decedent before his death was covered by that policy.

 **DECEDENT ON MEDICARE**

If the decedent was covered by Medicare, you do not need to notify anyone, but you do need to know what things were covered by Medicare so that you can determine what medical bills are (or are not) covered by Medicare. The government publication MEDICARE AND YOU (Publication No. CMS-10050) explains what things are covered under Medicare and the different kinds of plans that are currently available. You can get the publication by writing to:

U.S. Dept. of Health and Human Services
Centers for Medicare and Medicaid Services
7500 Security Boulevard
Baltimore, MD 21244-1850

You can download the publication from the Internet.

 MEDICARE WEBSITE
http://www.medicare.gov

The publication is available on Audiotape, in Braille, in large print and in Spanish. To receive a copy you can call (800) 633-4227. TTY users call (877) 486-2048.

SPOUSE ▸ THE SPOUSE'S HEALTH INSURANCE

If the spouse of the decedent is insured under Medicare, then the death does not affect the surviving spouse's coverage. If the spouse was not covered by Medicare but has her own health insurance that also covered the decedent, then the spouse needs to notify the employer of the death because this may affect the cost of the plan to the employer and/or the spouse. If the spouse was covered under the decedent's policy then he/she needs to arrange for new coverage. There are state and federal laws that ensure continued coverage under the decedent's policy for a period of time depending on whether the decedent's employer falls under federal or state regulation.

If the decedent was employed by a federally regulated company (usually a company with at least twenty employees) then under the Consolidated Omnibus Budget Reconciliation Act ("COBRA") the employer must make the company health plan available to the surviving spouse and any dependent child of the decedent for at least 36 months. The employer is required to give notice to the surviving spouse that the spouse and/or dependent child have the right to continue coverage under the decedent's health plan. The spouse and/or child have 60 days from the date of death or 60 days after the employer sends notice (whichever is later) to tell the employer whether the surviving spouse and child wish to continue with the health insurance plan (29 U.S.C. Sec. 1162, 1163, 1165). The only problem with continued coverage may be the cost. Before the death, the employer may have been paying some percentage of the premium. The employer has no such duty after the death unless there was some employment agreement stating otherwise.

Under COBRA, the employer may charge the spouse for the full cost of the plan plus a 2% administrative fee. If you have a question about your coverage under COBRA, you can call the U.S. Department of Labor ("DOL") at (800) 998-7542 and ask for the number of your local DOL office.

You can also ask that they send you their publication **HEALTH BENEFITS UNDER COBRA**; or you can visit their Website for more information.

 U.S. DEPARTMENT OF LABOR
http://www.dol.gov/

HEALTH INSURANCE COVERAGE UNDER STATE LAW
The ARIZONA HEALTH CARE COST CONTAINMENT SYSTEM ADMINISTRATION is in charge of health care group programs within the state (ARS 36-2912). If you find you are no longer eligible for coverage under the decedent's health insurance plan, you can get information about coverage that may be available to you by calling (800) 325-2548 or by visiting the Arizona Department of Insurance Website.

 THE ARIZONA DEPT. OF INSURANCE
http://www.id.state.az.us

NOTIFY ADVERTISERS

Probably the last one in the world to learn of the decedent's death is the direct mail advertiser. Advertisers are nothing if not tenacious. It is not uncommon for advertisements to be mailed to the decedent for more than ten years after the death. It is not because the advertiser is trying to sell something to the decedent, but rather the people who prepare (and sell) mailing lists do not know that the person is dead.

Those who sell mailing lists may not be motivated to update the list because of the cost of doing the necessary research; and perhaps because the price of the mailing list is often based on the number of people on the list. Even those who compose their own list may decide it is less costly to mail to everyone, than take the time (and money) to update the list.

If it gives you pleasure to think of advertisers spending substantial sums for nothing, then that is what you should do (nothing). But for those of you who wince each time you see another piece of mail addressed to the decedent, you can write to the Direct Marketing Association and ask that the name be deleted from all mailing lists:

> Mail Preference Service
> Direct Marketing Association
> P.O. Box 9008
> Farmingdale, NY 11735

You will need to give them the decedent's complete address, including zip code and every name variation that the decedent may have used; for example:

Theodore James Jones	T. J. Jones
Ted Jones	Ted J. Jones
T. James Jones	Jim Jones, etc.

CHANGE BENEFICIARIES

If the decedent was someone you named as beneficiary of your insurance policy, Will, Trust, brokerage account or pension plan, then you may need to name another beneficiary in his place:

INSURANCE POLICY

If you named the decedent as the primary beneficiary of your life insurance policy, check to see whether you named a *contingent* (alternate) beneficiary in the event that the decedent did not survive you. If not, you need to contact the insurance company and name a new beneficiary. If you did name a contingent beneficiary, that person is now your primary beneficiary and you need to consider whether you wish to name a new contingent beneficiary at this time.

HEALTH INSURANCE POLICY

If the decedent was covered under your health insurance policy, your employer and the health insurer need to be notified of the death because this may affect the cost of the plan to you and/or your employer.

WILL OR TRUST

Most Wills provide for a contingent beneficiary in the event that the person named as beneficiary dies first. If you named the decedent as your beneficiary, check to see whether you named an alternate beneficiary. If not, you need to have your attorney revise your Will and name a new beneficiary.

Similarly, if you are the Settlor (or Grantor) of a Trust and the decedent was one of the beneficiaries of your Trust, check the Trust document to see if you named an alternate beneficiary. If not, contact your attorney to prepare an amendment to the Trust, naming a new beneficiary.

BANK AND SECURITIES ACCOUNTS ✍

If the decedent was a beneficiary or joint owner of your bank or securities account, you may wish to arrange for a new beneficiary or joint owner at this time.

PENSION PLANS ✍

If the decedent was a beneficiary under your pension plan, you need to notify them of his death and name a new beneficiary. Many pension plans require that you notify them within a set period of time (usually 30 days from the date of death), so it is important to notify them as soon as you are able. If the decedent was a beneficiary of your Individual Retirement Account ("IRA") or of your Qualified Retirement Plan ("QRP") and you did not provide for an alternate beneficiary, you need to name another.

Before you choose an alternate beneficiary, it is important that you understand all of the options available to you. Not an easy task. There are many complex government regulations relating to IRA and QRP accounts. Even if you believe you understood your options when you set up your account, the federal government often changes those options.

Your choice of beneficiary might impact the amount of money you can withdraw each month, so it is important to consult with your accountant, tax attorney or financial planner, before you make your election.

NOTIFYING CREDITORS

It is the job of the person appointed as Personal Representative to notify the decedent's creditors of the death so that the creditor is given an opportunity to come forward and file a *claim* (a written demand for payment) for monies owed. The attorney for the Personal Representative usually takes care of the notice procedure. We will explain that procedure later in this book.

If no Probate proceeding is necessary, the next of kin can notify the creditors of the death, but before doing so, it is important to read Chapter 4: WHAT BILLS NEED TO BE PAID? That chapter explains what bills need to be paid and who is responsible to pay them.

Before any bill can be paid, you need to know whether the decedent left any asset that can be used to pay those debts. The next chapter explains how to identify, and then locate all of the property owned by the decedent.

Locating the Assets 3

It is important to locate the financial records of the decedent and then carefully examine those records. Even the partner of a long-term marriage should conduct a thorough search because the surviving spouse may be unaware of all that was owned (or owed) by the decedent.

It is not unusual for a surviving spouse to be surprised when learning of the decedent's business transactions, especially in those cases where the decedent had control of family finances. One such example is that of Sam and Henrietta. They married just as soon as Sam was discharged from the army after World War II. During their marriage, Sam handled all of the finances giving Henrietta just enough money to run the household.

Every now and again Henrietta would think of getting a job. She longed to have her own source of income and some economic independence. Each time she brought up the subject Sam would loudly object. He had no patience for this new "woman's lib" thing. Sam said he got married to have a real wife — one who would cook his meals and keep house for him.

Henrietta was not the arguing type. She rationalized, saying that Sam had a delicate stomach and dust allergies. He needed her to prepare his special meals and keep an immaculate house for him. Besides, Sam had a good job with a major cruise line and he needed her to accompany him on his frequent business trips.

Once Sam retired, he was even more cautious in his spending habits. Henrietta seldom complained. She assumed the reason for his "thrift" was that they had little money and had to live on his pension.

They were married 52 years when Sam died at the age of 83. Henrietta was 81 at the time of his death. She was one very happy, very angry and very aged widow when she discovered that Sam left her with assets worth well over a million dollars!

LOCATING RECORDS

As you go through the papers of the decedent you may come across documents that indicate property ownership, such as bank registers, stock or bond certificates, insurance policies, pension or annuity records, etc. Place all evidence of ownership in a single place. You will need to contact the different companies in order to transfer title to the proper beneficiary.

To obtain the property, you may need to produce evidence of the decedent's personal relationships, such as a marriage or birth certificate, or naturalization papers, or military personnel records. If you cannot locate the decedent's marriage or birth certificate, you can get a copy of those records from the Vital Records office in the state where the event took place. Many states (including Arkansas) restrict access to these records to the decedent's Personal Representative or to close family members (ARS 36-324). See Chapter 1 for the telephone number of the Vital Records Officer for Arizona. You can use the Internet to locate vital records in other states by using your favorite search engine to find Vital Statistics or Vital Records in that state.

MILITARY RECORDS: The next of kin can obtain a copy of the military record of a deceased veteran by writing to:

The National Personnel Records Center
Military Personnel Records
9700 Page Avenue
St. Louis, MO   63132-5100

They will send you form SF 180 to complete. You can fax your request to them at (314) 801-9195, or you can download the form from the Internet.

 National Archives and Records Administration
http://www.vetrecs.archives.gov

COLLECT AND IDENTIFY KEYS

The decedent may have kept his records in a safe deposit box, so you may find that your first job is to locate the keys to the box. As you go through the personal effects of the decedent, collect and identify all the keys that you find. If you come across an unidentified key, it could be a key to a post office box (private or federal) or a safe deposit box located in a bank or in a private vault company. You will need to determine whether that key opens a box that contains property belonging to the decedent or whether the key is to a box no longer in use. Some ways to investigate are as follows:

☑ CHECK BUSINESS RECORDS

If the decedent kept receipts, look through those items to see if he paid for the rental of a post office or safe deposit box. Also, look at his check register to see if he wrote a check to the Postmaster or to any safe deposit or vault company. Look at his bank statements to see if there is any bank charge for a safe deposit box. Some banks bill separately for safe deposit boxes so check with all of the banks in which the decedent had an account to determine if he had a safe deposit box with that bank.

☑ CHECK THE KEY TYPE

If you cannot identify the key, take it to a local locksmith and ask whether anyone can identify the type of facility that uses such keys. If that doesn't work, go to each bank, post office and private safe deposit box company where the decedent shopped, worked or frequented and ask whether they use the type of key that you found.

☑ CHECK THE MAIL

Check the mail over the next several months to see if the decedent receives a statement requesting payment for the next year's rental of a post office or safe deposit box.

FORWARD THE DECEDENT'S MAIL

You may find evidence of a brokerage account, bank account, or safe deposit box by examining correspondence addressed to the decedent. If he was living alone, have his mail forwarded to the person he named as Personal Representative or Executor of his Will. If the decedent did not leave a Will, and Probate is not necessary, forward the mail to his next of kin. Call the Postmaster and ask him to send you the necessary forms to make the change. Request that the mail be forwarded for the longest period allowed by law (currently one year).

Instead of calling, you can download the change of address form from the U.S. Post Office Website.

 U.S. POST OFFICE
http://www.uspo.com

THE POST OFFICE BOX RENTAL
The decedent may have been renting a post office box at his local post office branch or perhaps at the branch closest to where he did his banking. Ask the Postmaster to help you determine whether the decedent was renting a post office box. If so, you need to locate the key to the box so that you can collect the decedent's mail.

LOST POST OFFICE BOX KEY
If the decedent had a post office box and you cannot locate the key, contact the postmaster and ask him to give you the necessary forms to complete in order to get possession of the mail in that box.

As before, have all mail addressed to that box forwarded to the Personal Representative, or if Probate is not necessary, to the decedent's next of kin.

WHAT TO DO WITH CHECKS

You may receive checks in the mail made out to the decedent. Social Security checks, pension checks and annuity checks issued after the date of death may need to be returned to the sender. (See pages -- and -- of this book.) Other checks need to be deposited. If Probate is necessary, the Personal Representative will open a Probate Estate account and deposit the decedent's checks to that account.

If Probate is not necessary, checks can be deposited to any account held in the name of the decedent. The decedent is not here to endorse the check, but you can deposit it to his account by writing his bank account number on the back of the check and printing beneath it **FOR DEPOSIT ONLY.**

The bank will accept such an endorsement and deposit the check into the decedent's account. The account can then be transferred to the proper beneficiarfy using an appropriate transfer procedure as described later in Chapter 6.

If the check is significant in value or the decedent had different accounts that are accessible to different people, then there needs to be cooperation and a sense of fair play. If not, the dollar gain may not nearly offset the emotional turmoil. That was the case with Gail. Her father made her a joint owner of his checking account to assist in paying his bills. He had macular degeneration and it was increasingly difficult for him to see. The father also had a savings account that was in his name only.

Gail's brother Ken had a good paying job in Alaska. Even though he lived at a distance, Ken, his wife and two children always spent the Christmas holidays with his father and sister.

Each summer, their father enjoyed leaving the heat of Arizona to spend a few weeks in the cool Alaskan climate.

One summer, the father purchased a round trip ticket to Alaska. It cost several hundred dollars. Just before the departure date, the father had a heart attack and died. Gail called the airline to cancel the ticket. They refunded the money in a check made out to her father. She deposited the check to the joint account, and then closed it out.

As part of the Probate procedure, the money in the father's savings account was divided equally between Ken and his sister. Ken wondered what happened to the money from the airline tickets.

Gail explained "Dad paid for the tickets from the joint account, so I deposited the money back to that account. "

"Aren't you going to give me half?"

"Dad meant for me to have whatever was in that joint account. If he wanted you to have half of the money, he would have made you joint owner as well."

Ken didn't see it that way "That refund was part of Dad's Estate. It should have been deposited to his savings account to be divided equally between us. Are you going to force me to argue this in Court?"

Gail finally agreed to split the money with Ken, but the damage was done.

Gail complains that holidays are lonely since Dad died.

LOCATE FINANCIAL RECORDS

To locate the decedent's assets you need to find evidence of what he owned and where those assets are located. His financial records should lead you to the location of all of his assets, so your first job is to locate those records. The best place to start the search is in the decedent's home. Many people keep their financial records in a single place but it is important to check the entire house to be sure you did not miss something.

CHECK THE COMPUTER

Don't overlook that computer sitting silently in the corner. It may hold the decedent's check register and all of his financial records. You may want to monitor his E-mail for E-bank or credit card accounts.

The computer may be programmed to protect this information. If you cannot access the decedent's financial records, you may need to employ a computer technician or computer consultant who will be able to print out all of the information on the hard drive of the computer. You can find such a technician or consultant by looking in the telephone book under COMPUTER SUPPORT SERVICES or COMPUTER SYSTEM DESIGNS & CONSULTANTS.

LOCATE TITLE TO WATERCRAFT

Arizona Game and Fish is in charge of the registration of watercraft operated within the state. All motorized watercraft operated within the state must be registered (ARS 5-322). You should find the Certificate of Number giving the number issued by the Department. That number should be prominently displayed on the boat. If you cannot locate the Certificate of Number, you can call the Arizona Game and Fish at (602) 942-3000.

LOCATE TITLE TO MOTOR VEHICLE

If the decedent owned a motor vehicle you need to locate the title to the vehicle and its registration. If you cannot find the title certificate you can go to the Motor Vehicle Office in the county of the decedent's residence and they will issue a replacement (duplicate) title to you. The Motor Vehicle Office will require proof of your authority to get a copy of the Title. In some cases, they will issue the replacement title only to the Personal Representative.

It is a good idea to first call and ask what information they require and the cost of obtaining the replacement Title.
            Phoenix (602) 255-0072   Tucson (520) 629-9808
              Elsewhere in Arizona (800) 324-5425
                 TDD Service: (800) 324-5425

If you find there is a loan on the car, contact the lienholder and get a copy of the contract that is the basis of the loan.

THE LEASED CAR

You may find that the car is leased and not owned by the decedent. If so, contact the lessor and get a copy of the lease agreement. Check to see whether the decedent had life insurance as part of the agreement. If he did, then the lease may now be paid in full and the beneficiary of the car should be able to use the car for the remainder of the leasing period, or take title to the car, whichever option is available under the lease agreement. The Personal Representative (or the beneficiary) can send the death certificate to the leasing company with a copy of the contract and a letter requesting that the transfer be made. If the lease is not paid in full upon the decedent's death, arrangements need to be made to satisfy the terms of the agreement. See Chapter 6 for information about transferring a leased car.

LOCATE TITLE TO MOBILE/MANUFACTURED HOME

A motorized home that is not permanently attached to real property is considered to be personal property. It is titled and registered in the same manner as a motor vehicle. A **mobile** or **manufactured home** is a structure that is built on a permanent chassis (i.e. supporting frame). It is transportable in one or more sections. It designed for use as a dwelling, with or without a permanent foundation, when connected to the required utilities (ARS 33-1409).

Once a mobile/manufactured home is permanently affixed to a parcel of land, the owner signs an *Affidavit of Affixture* and surrenders his Certificate of Title to the Department of Transportation. The Department will issue a receipt for Certificate of Title. Once the Affidavit of Affixture is recorded, it is no longer necessary to follow the registration requirements of a motor vehicle. The mobile/manufactured home is registered with the County Assessor and is subject to property taxes as with any other residential property (ARS 28-2063).

If the decedent owned a parcel of land and his mobile/manufactured home was permanently attached to that land, then turn to Chapter 6 for information about transferring the land and the mobile home to the proper beneficiary. If the decedent owned a mobile home that is kept in a leased space, you need to locate the lease to the mobile home lot. If you cannot locate the lease, contact the landlord for a copy, and proceed in the same manner as for a residential lease.

Special
Situation

DECEDENT'S
RESIDENTIAL LEASE

If the decedent was renting his residence, he may have a written lease agreement. It is important to locate the lease because the decedent's Estate may be responsible for payments under the lease. If you cannot find a lease, ask the landlord for a copy. If he reports that there was no written lease, verify that the decedent was on a month to month basis and then work out a mutually agreeable time in which to vacate the premises.

If a written lease is in effect, determine the end of the lease period, and whether the landlord is holding a security deposit. Ask whether he will agree to cancel the lease on condition that the property is promptly vacated and left in good condition. If the landlord wants to hold the Estate responsible to pay the balance of the lease, have your attorney review the lease to determine what rights and responsibilities remain now that the tenant is deceased.

 **LAWYER**

DECEDENT'S
ONGOING BUSINESS

If the decedent was the sole owner of a business, or if he owned a partnership interest in a business, the Personal Representative needs to take possession of the decedent's business records and make arrangements for the operation of the business. The company accountant or company lawyer may be able to assist in obtaining the records. If you are a beneficiary of the Estate, consider consulting with your own attorney to determine what rights and responsibilities you may have in the business.

If the decedent owned an aircraft, you should find a certificate of title to the aircraft. The Aircraft Registration Branch of the Federal Aviation Administration ("FAA") maintains aircraft records. The Aircraft Registration Branch is located in Oklahoma City, Oklahoma. Aircraft records are open to the general public, but researching the documents yourself may be difficult because the records are maintained by the registration number of the aircraft, and the Aircraft Registration Branch does not furnish lien information or the names of previous owners.

The Aircraft Registration Branch does not perform title searches, however they can give you a list of title search companies. You can call them toll free at (866) 835-5322, or visit their Website for a list of title companies.

 THE FEDERAL AVIATION ADMINISTRATION
http://www.faa.gov

In addition to locating title to the aircraft, you need to find the FAA registration and the Arizona registration. Arizona statute requires that all aircraft be registered with the FAA and with the Aeronautics Division of the Arizona Department of transportation (ARS 28-8272, 28-8322). Once the registration fee, and license tax are paid to the Arizona Department of Transportation, they will issue a certificate and a License Decal (ARS 28-8325).

The License Decal should be prominently displayed on the aircraft. If you cannot locate the certificate issued by the Arizona Department of Transportation, you can call the Aeronautics Division of the Department of Transportation at (602) 294-9144 for information about obtaining a replacement certificate.

COLLECT DEEDS

Collect deeds to all of the property owned by the decedent. In addition to the deed, look for other documents associated with the property, such as a mortgage. You may come across a Title Insurance policy. The new owner might be able to turn in that policy and receive a discount toward the purchase of a new title insurance, so it is important to keep the policy together with the deed. Instead of a title insurance policy you may find an *Abstract of Title*. An Abstract of Title is a summary of the documents and facts appearing on the public record which affect title to the property. The Abstract will need to be updated once the property is transferred. We will discuss the transfer of property in Chapter 6.

Many people keep deeds in a safe deposit box. If you cannot find the deed in the decedent's home, determine whether he had a safe deposit box and if so, you need to examine the contents of the box. See the end of this chapter for information about how to access the decedent's safe deposit box.

If you know that the decedent owned real property (lot, residential property, condominium) but you cannot find the deed, contact the County Recorder in the county where the property is located. He can provide you with a copy of the last recorded deed. The Recorder may ask you to identify the parcel of land by giving the legal description of the land or its parcel identification number. You can find this information on the last tax bill sent to the decedent. If you cannot find the last tax bill, call the County Assessor's office and they will give you the information. You can find a listing of all Tax Assessors in Arizona on the Internet. http://www.searchsystems.net.

You need to locate the deed and any related document (Abstract of Title, title insurance policy, recorded condominium approval, etc.) to out of state property owned by the decedent.

THE LOST OUT OF STATE DEED

If you know the decedent owned out of state real property, but cannot find the deed, you can use the same procedure just described, namely, you can check with the recording department in the county where the property is located. In some states the Clerk of the Circuit Court is in charge of the recording department. In other states, it may be the Registrar of Deeds. The Clerk in the recording department should be able to give you a copy of the last recorded deed.

Many states index the property by the name of the current owner of the property, so if you know the county where the property is located, you should be able to find the deed by giving the decedent's name to the Clerk.

If you do not know the county in which the property is located, you will need to wait for the next tax bill. The tax bill should contain its legal description and/or tax identification number.

COLLECT TAX RECORDS

The decedent's final federal and state income tax return needs to be filed. To prepare these return you may need to refer to the returns he filed for the past three years. If you cannot locate his prior tax records, check his personal telephone book and/or his personal bank register to see if he employed someone to prepare his taxes. His tax preparer should have a copy of those records.

If you are unable to locate the decedent's federal tax returns, they can be obtained from the IRS. The IRS will send copies of the decedent's tax filings to anyone who has a *fiduciary relationship* with the decedent. The IRS considers the following people to be a fiduciary:

➤ the person appointed as the Personal Representative of the decedent's Estate

➤ the Successor Trustee of the decedent's Trust

➤ if the person died ***intestate,*** (without a Will), whoever is legally entitled to possession of the decedent's property (See Chapter 5 for an explanation of the Laws of Intestate Succession).

The fiduciary can receive copies of the decedent's tax filings by notifying IRS that he/she is acting in a fiduciary capacity, and then requesting the copies. To notify the IRS of the fiduciary capacity file Form 56:
NOTICE CONCERNING FIDUCIARY RELATIONSHIP
To request a copy of the tax return file Form 4506:
REQUEST FOR A COPY OF TAX RETURN

Your accountant can file these forms for you or you can obtain the forms from the IRS by calling (800) 829-3676 or you can download them from the FORMS section of the IRS Website.

 INTERNAL REVENUE SERVICE
http://www.irs.gov

LOCATE STATE INCOME TAX RETURN

The Personal Representative, or whoever is entitled to possession of the decedent's property, will need to file the state income tax return at the same time the federal income tax return is filed (ARS 43-325). You may need last year's return to help prepare the final return. If you cannot locate the decedent's state income tax return you can obtain copies from the Arizona Department of Revenue. To get a copy of the decedent's state income tax return, you need to fill out a form entitled:

Notice Of Assumption of Fiduciary Duties

and Arizona Form 450:

Request for Certified Copies of Document.

To obtain a copy of these forms, call the state form order department at (602) 542-4260 or you can fax your request to (602) 542-3756 , or you can write to:

Arizona Department of Revenue
Forms Order Department
1600 W. Monroe
Phoenix, AZ   85007-2650

or you can download the forms from the Internet.

http://www.azdor.gov

LOCATE OUT OF STATE ACCOUNTS

If the decedent had an out of state bank or brokerage account, you might be able to locate the account through its monthly or quarterly statements. Not all financial institutions send out statements on a regular basis; however, all institutions are required to send out IRS tax form 1099 at the end of the year giving the amount of interest or dividend earned on that account. Once the forms come in, you will learn the location of the decedent's accounts that were active during the year.

If the decedent was forgetful, he may have money in a lost bank account or abandoned safe deposit box. Property that is unclaimed is turned over to the Arizona Department of Revenue after a period of time as set by Arizona law. The time period depends on the item:.

- ⌛ 1 year for unclaimed wages
- ⌛ 1 year after the expiration of the lease on a safe deposit box
- ⌛ 5 years from the last transaction on a bank account
- ⌛ 5 years after monies are payable under a life insurance policy or annuity
- ⌛ 7 years for a money order
- ⌛ 15 years from the date of issue of a travelers check (ARS 44-302, 44-303).

Once the property is turned over to the Department of Revenue, they will try to locate the owner by publishing a notice in a newspaper of general circulation giving the name and last known address of the owner of the property (ARS 44-309).

You can determine whether there is a record identifying the decedent as the owner of abandoned property by calling (602) 364-0380 or by writing to:

THE DEPARTMENT OF REVENUE
UNCLAIMED PROPERTY UNIT
P.O. Box 29026
Phoenix, AZ   85038-9026

You can also get information from the Internet.

 ARIZONA UNCLAIMED PROPERTY
http://www.azdor.gov/ucp

CLAIMS IN OTHER STATES

Each state has an agency or department that is responsible for handling unclaimed property within that state. If the decedent had residences in other states, call the **UNCLAIMED PROPERTY** department of the state Comptroller or Treasurer to see if the decedent has unclaimed property in that state.

EAGLE PUBLISHING COMPANY OF BOCA lists telephone numbers for the unclaimed property division for each state at the Public Information section of its Website.

http://www.eaglepublishing.com

CLAIMS FOR DECEDENT VICTIMS OF HOLOCAUST

The New York State Banking Department has a special Claims Processing Office for Holocaust survivors or their heirs. The office processes claims for Swiss bank accounts that were dormant since the end of World War II. If the decedent was a victim of the Holocaust, you can get information about money that may be due to the decedent's Estate by calling (800) 695-3318.

UNCLAIMED INCOME TAX REFUNDS

The IRS reports that each year they are unable to deliver thousands of income tax refund checks, mostly because a taxpayer moves and neglects to notify the IRS, or the U.S. Postal Service of their new address. In addition to undeliverable income tax refunds, many people are entitled to a refund but no check is sent because they fail to file an income tax return. This is often the case with employees who earned too little income to file a tax return. They may not be aware that taxes withheld from their wages are refundable. Other employees may not have had any tax withheld, but if they had a low income they might be eligible for an Earned Income Tax Credit, provided they file an income tax return. The IRS gives taxpayers three years to claim these funds. There is no penalty for filing a late return in order to qualify for these refunds.

You can determine whether the decedent is entitled to an income tax refund or a Earned Income Tax Credit by calling the IRS at (800) 829-1040. You can also get information about unclaimed tax refunds by visiting the IRS Website.
http://www.irs.gov/

UNCLAIMED STATE TAX REFUNDS

The Arizona Department of Revenue also reports that thousands of tax refunds are returned to them each year by the U.S. Postal Service marked "undeliverable." To determine whether the decedent is entitled to an Arizona income tax refund call the Arizona Department of Revenue at (602) 255-3381 or you can write to them at:

ARIZONA DEPARTMENT OF REVENUE
Taxpayer Information & Assistance
1600 W. Monroe
Phoenix, AZ   85008-2650

THE LOST PENSION

The decedent may be entitled to benefits under a pension plan of a prior employer. If the decedent worked for an employer for any significant period of time, say five years or more, check with the company benefit representative to determine whether any pension funds are owed to the decedent. If you are unable to locate the former employer, it could be that the company moved or merged with another company. There are several ways to track down the company, starting with the Corporation Commission, to learn of the company's current status (see page 50).

CONTACT THE UNION
If the decedent belonged to a union, contact them and ask them to help you locate the company. They may be able to tell you whether the company is still in business, and if not, what happened to the company's pension funds.

CONTACT SOCIAL SECURITY
The Social Security Administration has the decedent's work record and the employer identification number for each of his employers. The Personal Representative can get this information by calling the Social Security Administration at (800) 772-1213.

RESEARCH THE INTERNET
Pension Benefit Guaranty Corporation insures private sector pensions. They operate an on-line search tool for those employees who did not collect their pension because the company became bankrupt or dissolved the plan, or because the company could not locate the employee. You can search their Website by employee name or by the company name.

 PENSION BENEFIT GUARANTY CORPORATION
http://www.pbgc.gov/search

LOCATE CONTRACTS

HEALTH CLUB CONTRACT

If the decedent belonged to a health club or gym, he may have prepaid for the year. Look for the club contract. It will give the terms of the agreement. If you cannot locate the contract, then contact the company for a copy of the agreement. If the contract was prepaid, then determine whether the agreement provides for a refund for the unused portion.

Even if the contract does not provide for a refund, you may be able to get the owner of the gym to agree to assigning the remaining membership to an heir of the decedent's Estate. Such an assignment is good public relations as well as a means of generating new business should the heir decide to purchase his own membership.

SERVICE CONTRACT

Many people purchase appliance service contracts to have their appliances serviced in the event that an appliance should need repair. If the decedent had a security system, he may have had a service contract with a company to monitor the system and contact the police in the event of a break-in.

If the decedent had a service contract, then you need to locate it and determine whether it can be assigned to the new owner of the property. If the contract is assignable, the new owner can reimburse the decedent's Estate for the unused portion. If the contract cannot be assigned, then once the property is transferred, try to obtain a refund for the unused portion of the contract.

Upon notice of the death, whoever has possession of the decedent's original Will needs to deposit it with the Registrar in the county of the decedent's residence. The office of the Registrar is located in the Probate section of the Superior Court (ARS 14-3201). You can call the Registrar's office for directions or you can find that information on the Internet at the Court Locator section of the Arizona Supreme Court Website.

ARIZONA COURTS
http://www.supreme.state.az.us

The Registrar will accept an original Will only and not a copy, so it is important to hand carry the original document to the Court. If you are the Executor or Personal Representative named in the Will, you can give the Will to your attorney to file with the Court when he begins the Probate procedure. Make a copy of the Will for your records before delivering it to the Court or to your attorney, but don't alter the Will by removing its staples.

If you believe that Probate is not necessary, it is still a good idea to promptly deposit the Will with the Registrar. He will keep it on file with the Probate Court in the event it turns out that Probate is necessary at some later date. If an interested party asks you to deposit the Will with the Court and for some reason, you fail to do so, you may be held liable for any harm caused by your failure.

If the decedent owned property in Arizona, but did not live here, the Will may be deposited with the Probate Court in the county where the decedent's property is located. However, before doing so, read the next page.

 **LAWYER**

PROBATING THE OUT OF STATE PROPERTY

If the decedent had his residence in Arizona and owned property in another state, you need to conduct the initial Probate in Arizona and an *ancillary* (secondary) Probate in the other state. If his residence was in another state and he owned property in Arizona, it may need to be the other way around; namely, you may need to conduct the initial Probate in the other state (ARS 14-3201).

If you are going to be Personal Representative, and the decedent owned property in another state or was a resident of another state, before depositing the Will with the Court consult with an experienced Probate attorney <u>in each state</u> to determine where the initial Probate should be conducted. Convenience is important, but there are other things you need to consider.

COST OF PROBATE
Ask each attorney whether the location of the initial Probate procedure will have an effect on the total cost of Probate.

WHO INHERITS THE INTESTATE ESTATE
Intestate laws vary significantly state to state. If the decedent died without a Will, it is important to determine whether the location of the initial Probate procedure will change the amount each heir will inherit.

ESTATE/INHERITANCE TAXES
Determine whether the location of the initial procedure will have an impact on the amount of taxes that need to be paid.

> ### Special Situation

WILL DRAFTED IN ANOTHER STATE OR COUNTRY

A Will that was drafted in another state or country can be accepted into Probate in Arizona, provided:

☑ the Will was prepared and signed according to the laws of the state where it was drafted

- or -

☑ if the decedent was a resident of another state, the Will was prepared and signed according to the laws of that state

- or -

☑ the Will was prepared and signed in accordance with Arizona law (ARS 14-2506).

See Chapter 5 for a discussion of what constitutes a valid Will in the state of Arizona.

 **LAWYER**

WILL DRAFTED IN ANOTHER LANGUAGE

If the Will is written in a language other than English, you will need to have it translated. Consult with an attorney to determine what proof the judge will require in order to accept the translated Will into Probate as a true and correct translation of the original.

THE MISSING WILL

People tend to put off making a Will until they think they need to. For many, that need arises when they are elderly and/or seriously ill and have property that they want to leave to someone. It is uncommon for a young person to have a Will; but those who are aged, and with significant assets, usually have one.

A survey conducted for the American Association of Retired Persons ("AARP") found that the probability of having a Will increases with age. Forty-four percent of those surveyed who were between the ages of 50 to 54 had a Will. This increased to 85% for those 80 and older. You can find details of the survey at the AARP Website.

 AMERICAN ASSOCIATION OF RETIRED PERSONS
http://www.research.aarp.org

Those who make a Will usually tell the person they appoint as Executor of the existence of the Will. Chances are, that someone in the decedent's circle of family and friends, knows whether there is a Will. If you believe that the decedent had a Will, but you cannot find it, then there are at least three places to check out:

⇨ THE REGISTRAR OF THE PROBATE COURT
Whoever has the original Will should deposit it with the Probate Court as soon as that person learns of the death. It is a good idea to check with the Registrar in the county where the decedent lived in the chance that someone found the Will and filed it with the Court.

⇨ **THE DECEDENT'S ATTORNEY**

Look at the decedent's checkbook for the past few years and see whether he paid any attorney fees. If you are able to locate the decedent's attorney, call and inquire whether the attorney ever drafted a Will for the decedent, and if so, whether the attorney has the original Will in his possession. If he has the Will, ask him to forward it to the Probate Court in the county of the decedent's residence. Asking the attorney to forward the Will to the court does not obligate you to employ the attorney should you later find that you need the assistance of an attorney for the Probate administration.

⇨ **THE SAFE DEPOSIT BOX**

Most people keep their original Will in a safe deposit box. If you believe the decedent had a Will but you cannot find it, check to see if he had a safe deposit box. If he did, you will need to gain entry to that box to see whether the Will is in the box. See the page 86 for an explanation of how to gain entry to the safe deposit box.

A COPY OF THE WILL
AND NO ORIGINAL

A person can revoke his Will simply by destroying it i.e., by ripping it up, or by writing over it in such a manner as to indicate that the Will is cancelled or revoked (ARS 14-2507). If you have a copy of the Will and cannot find the original, the Probate judge will presume that the decedent revoked his Will by destroying it.

If you believe the original was not revoked but is lost, you can ask the Court to admit a copy of the Will to Probate. Arizona courts will allow a copy of a lost Will to be probated provided it can be proven that:

☑ the document offered is a true copy of the original Will
> AND

☑ the decedent did not revoke the Will. (ARS 14-3415).

Not easy things to prove. If you wish to have a lost Will admitted to Probate, you will need to employ an attorney experienced in Probate matters to present your case to the Court.

ACCESSING THE SAFE DEPOSIT BOX

If the decedent rented a safe deposit box with another person, each with free access to the box, the surviving joint renter of the box can go to the box and remove the contents of the box (ARS 6-1004). If the decedent was the only person with access to the safe deposit box, any interested party (spouse, family member, person named in the Will, etc.) can ask the bank (or safe deposit box lessor) to allow them to examine the contents of the box (ARS 6-1008).

If the bank allows inspection, at least two company employees must be present when the safe deposit box is opened. If the Will is found in the box, the bank can deliver it to the Clerk of the Superior Court. If the person named as Executor or Personal Representative is present, the bank may give the Will to that person. Also, under Arizona law, if an insurance policy is in the safe deposit box the bank may give the policy to the beneficiary named in the policy. Nothing else may be removed from the safe deposit box until someone provides proof to the bank that he is legally entitled to take possession of the contents of the safe deposit box.

While Arizona law gives the bank authority to allow inspection of the contents of the box, the statute does not require they do so. The bank has the right to deny inspections of the safe deposit box without authorization from the Probate Court. In most cases that authorization is in the form of Letters issued by that Court giving the Personal Representative the right to take possession of all of the decedent's property. The Personal Representative can access the safe deposit box as soon as the Court signs his Letters.

Before going to the bank to examine the contents of the decedent's safe deposit box, it is best to call ahead of time to determine whether they will allow the inspection. If they agree to do so, make an appointment to meet with an officer of the company. Most companies require that you bring a certified copy of the death certificate, so you may need to wait until you receive the death certificate to prove to the bank officials that the owner of the box is dead.

If you find valuables in the box that need to be removed from the box, you will need to go through some kind of Probate procedure to get possession of those items. See Chapter 6 for an explanation of what type of Probate procedure may be necessary to get possession of the contents of the decedent's safe deposit box.

Before leaving the bank, you may want to ask an officer of the company to make an inventory of the contents of the decedent's safe deposit box using the company letterhead. You may need the inventory to present to the court should you need an order to get possession of the contents of the box.

After examining the contents of the safe deposit box, determine whether it is necessary to keep the box open during the administration of the Estate, or whether the lease can be cancelled and monies refunded to the decedent's Estate.

Once you have located the decedent's property you may think the next step is to determine who gets to inherit that property. But some of that property may be needed to pay monies owed by the decedent; so the next step is to determine what, if any, bills need to be paid.

And that is the topic of the next chapter.

What Bills Need To Be Paid? 4

The Personal Representative has the duty to be sure that all valid claims against the Estate (demands for payment) are paid. If the decedent had debts, but no money or property, then of course, there is no way to pay the claim. The only remaining question is whether anyone else is responsible to pay for the monies owed. If the decedent was married, the first person the creditor will look to is the decedent's spouse. To understand the basis of this expectation, you need to know a bit of the history of our legal system.

Our laws are derived from the English Common Law. Under early English Common Law, a single woman had the right to own property in her own name and also the right to contract to buy or sell property; but when she married, her legal identity merged with her spouse. She could not hold property free from her husband's claim or control. She could no longer enter into a contract without her husband's permission.

Once married, a woman became financially dependent on her husband. He, in turn, became legally responsible to provide his wife with basic necessities — food, clothing, shelter and medical services. If anyone provided basic necessities to his wife, then regardless of whether the husband agreed to be responsible for the debt, he became obliged to pay for them. This law was called the DOCTRINE OF NECESSARIES.

The United States inherited its legal system from England, but over the years each state developed its own set of laws relating to spousal responsibility. Some states decided to make the Doctrine of Necessaries part of their state law. Other states, such as New Jersey, decided to apply the Doctrine equally to both sexes, making the husband responsible to pay for his wife's necessaries and the wife responsible to pay for her husband's necessaries. Other states, such as Florida, abolished the law altogether. In these states neither spouse is liable for the debts of the other unless the spouse agrees to pay the debt.

Things are more complicated in Arizona because it is a Community Property state. Whether the spouse is responsible to pay the decedent's debts depends on whether the property owned by the surviving spouse is COMMUNITY PROPERTY or SEPARATE PROPERTY.

COMMUNITY PROPERTY
Arizona statute 25-211 defines *Community Property* as property that is acquired by either husband or wife during the marriage — with the exception of property either party inherits or is given as a gift. If the couple lived in another state during the marriage, property either of them acquired is called *Quasi-community property* (ARS 25-318A).

Laws relating to Quasi-community property are much the same as those for Community property. For simplicity, we will use the term "Community Property" understanding that the law quoted applies to Quasi-community property as well.

SEPARATE PROPERTY

Separate property is defined as anything owned by a spouse prior to marriage and anything acquired by a spouse during the marriage as a gift or an inheritance. Any profit or increase in value of Separate Property is also Separate Property (ARS 25-213). For example, if a husband owned rental property prior to his marriage, then any money he receives as rental is Separate Property. If the property appreciates in value, that increase in value is also Separate Property. But if the increase in value of Separate Property is due to the efforts of the spouse, the spouse may be entitled to half of that increase in value.

THE COMMUNITY DEBT

Money spent for the benefit of the family or to manage or care for their family property is a **Community Debt** to be paid from the couple's Community Property. If there is not enough Community Property to pay the debt, whoever contracted for the goods or services must use his Separate Property to do so (ARS 25-215).

But would the spouse be responsible to use Separate Property pay for those debts, if he/she did not agree to pay for them? In other words does the Doctrine of Necessaries apply in Arizona? Surprisingly, the answer is "no." Arizona Courts ruled that the Doctrine of Necessaries does not apply in this state (*Phoenix Baptist Hospital v. Aiken*, 179 Ariz. 289 (App. 1994), 877 P.2d 1345). This case is interesting because the hospital argued that there is an Arizona criminal statute (ARS 13-3611) that requires a spouse to provide necessities. The Court ruled that criminal statutes do not apply to civil matters (i.e., a law suit brought by one citizen against the other), unless the legislature intended that it apply to civil matters as well. The Court ruled that there was no indication of such legislative intent in this case.

COMMUNITY DEBT VS. SEPARATE DEBT

In Arizona, neither partner is responsible to use their Separate Property to pay for the debts (or necessities) of the other unless they agree to do so; but all of their Community Property is available to pay a Community Debt, regardless of whether the non-contracting spouse agreed, or even knew about the debt.

Not so with a SEPARATE DEBT. A *Separate Debt* is monies owed by one of the partners prior to their marriage; or monies owed that in no way benefits the family. For example, if a spouse is convicted of a crime and must pay for the harm he caused. In such case, the amount contributed by the innocent spouse to their Community Property is not available to pay the debt, nor is any of the spouse's Separate Property (ARS 25-215).

THE RESPONSIBILITY OF THE SURVIVING SPOUSE

Now let's apply all this to determine whether the surviving spouse is responsible to pay for monies owed by the decedent.

SPOUSE AGREED TO PAY DEBT
If the surviving spouse agreed to be responsible for the debt, he/she must pay the debt from whatever assets he/she has, regardless of whether that property is Separate Property or Community Property.

SPOUSE DID NOT AGREE TO PAY DEBT

If the surviving spouse did not agree to pay the decedent's debt, then whether the creditor can collect depends on whether the decedent had any Separate Property. If the decedent did not own Separate Property, the creditor will look to the decedent's share of the Community Property for payment of a Community Debt.

The decedent's share of the Community Property must be used to pay his debts even if the debts were incurred before the marriage, and even if the debts were incurred outside the state of Arizona.

If all the surviving spouse owns is Separate Property, the creditor cannot force the surviving spouse to use those assets to pay the debt (ARS 25-215(A)).

 LAWYER

MUCH DEBT
NO SEPARATE PROPERTY

It is important to consult with an attorney if the decedent left a significant debt and Community Property only. The surviving spouse needs to know how much of their Community Property must be used to pay the debt. Theoretically, if the decedent came into the marriage with nothing and contributed little, there may be little, if any, Community Property available to pay his debts. No doubt a creditor will not see things that way.

Regardless of the amount of the decedent's contribution it is best to consult with a Probate attorney to determine how much of the Community Property is at risk to pay the decedent's debts.

NO COMMUNITY LIABILITY FOR
OUT OF STATE TAXES ON PENSION

If the decedent retired to Arizona and was receiving a pension check, or monies from a retirement plan from another state, then Arizona statute 33-1151 protects those pension funds from any income tax that the other state might levy against those funds. The other state can get a judgment for taxes owed in that state on pension funds received by the decedent while he was a resident of Arizona, but they will not be able to collect on it in Arizona.

This protection extends to the spouse and any dependent of the decedent. Specifically, if the spouse or someone who was dependent on the decedent, inherits all of the decedent's property, then the other state will not be able to collect their income tax from that inheritance. This protection does not extend to anyone else. If the decedent was single and without any dependent, his out of state taxes can be collected from his Estate.

JOINT PROPERTY BUT NO JOINT DEBT

Suppose all of the decedent's funds are held jointly with his spouse or a family member and the joint owner of the account did not agree to pay those debts? Can the creditor require that half of the joint funds be set aside to pay the debt?

In Arizona, the answer is "Yes." Arizona statute 14-6102 states that if there isn't enough money in the decedent's Estate to pay all his creditors and the cost of settling his Estate, the beneficiary must give the money from the decedent's share of a joint account to the decedent's Personal Representative to the extent those monies are needed to pay such debts. Similarly, if the decedent had an account and he gave written instructions to the bank to pay the money to a beneficiary when he dies (a *"pay on death"* or an *"in trust for"* account), those funds are also available to pay the decedent's creditors.

If the joint owner or beneficiary of the account takes the money and it is needed to pay the decedent's debts, then as much as is necessary to pay the debt must be returned.

There is no obligation to turn over these funds unless a creditor writes to the Personal Representative demanding that the monies from the account be used to pay the debt. Once the Personal Representative receives the demand, then unless the beneficiary agrees to return the funds, the Personal Representative will start a court proceeding to recover the funds. If he doesn't do so within two years from the decedent's date of death, the beneficiaries are free to keep the money (ARS 14-3803).

NO MONEY — NO PROPERTY

If the decedent owed money then the debt needs to be paid from assets owned by the decedent — which leads to the next question "Did the decedent have any money in his own name when he died?"

If the decedent died without any money or property in his name, then there is no money to pay any creditor. The only question that remains is whether anyone else is liable to pay those bills. The issue of payment most often arises in relation to services provided by nursing homes. When a person enters a nursing home, he is usually too ill to speak for himself or even sign his name. In such cases, the nursing home administrator may ask the spouse or family member to sign a battery of papers on behalf of the patient before allowing the patient to enter the facility. Buried in that battery of papers may be a statement that the family member agrees to be responsible for payment to the nursing home. If the family member refuses to guarantee payment and the patient's finances are limited, then the facility may refuse to admit the patient.

Under the Federal Nursing Home Reform Law, a nursing home that accepts Medicare or Medicaid payments is prohibited from requiring a family member to guarantee payment as a condition of allowing the patient to enter that facility (42 U.S.C. 13951-3(c)(5)(A)(ii)). Nonetheless, it is common practice for a nursing home, in effect, to say "Either someone agrees to pay for the patient's bill or you need to find a different facility."

Their position is understandable, in light of the fact that even if the patient is married, the nursing home cannot require payment from the spouse's Separate Property unless the spouse agrees to be responsible for monies owed. Most nursing homes are business establishments and not charitable organizations. The nursing home must be paid for the services they provide or they soon will be out of business. For an insolvent patient, the solution to the problem is to have the patient admitted to a facility as a Medicaid patient.

But suppose the decedent had some money when he entered the nursing home and you agreed to guarantee payment to the nursing home. What if you feel that you were coerced into signing as a guarantor?

Are you now liable to pay the decedent's final nursing home bill if your family member died without funds?

An experienced Elder Law attorney should be able to answer these questions after examining the documents that you signed and the conditions under which the patient entered the nursing home.

PAYING THE DECEDENT'S BILLS

If the decedent was married and Probate is not necessary, the surviving spouse needs to make provision for paying bills they were both responsible to pay. If the decedent was not married and he owned property belonging to him alone, such as a bank account, securities or real property, then paying monies owed by the decedent falls to the Personal Representative.

Just as soon as he is appointed, the Representative is required to make a diligent effort to locate all of the decedent's creditors and notify them that they have four months to file a claim against the decedent's Estate (ARS 14-3801).

The Personal Representative needs to look over each claim and decide whether that claim is valid. The problem with making that decision is that the decedent is not here to say whether he actually received the goods and services that are now being billed to his Estate.

That is especially the case for medical or nursing care bills. An example of improper billing brought to the attention of this author was that of a bill submitted for a physical examination of the decedent. The bill listed the date of the examination as July 10th, but the decedent died on July 9th. Other incorrect billings may not be as obvious, so each invoice needs to be carefully examined.

If the Personal Representative decides to challenge a bill, and is unable to settle the matter with the creditor, then the Probate court will decide whether the debt is valid and should be paid.

MEDICAL BILLS COVERED BY INSURANCE

If the decedent had health insurance you may receive an invoice stamped "THIS IS NOT A BILL." This means the health care provider has submitted the bill to the decedent's health insurance company and expects to be paid by them. If the decedent was receiving Medicare, you will receive a *Medicare Summary Notice* listing all of the services or supplies that were billed to Medicare for the prior 30 days. If the decedent was receiving Medicare Part B drugs, such as certain cancer drugs, you may receive two Medicare Summary Notices, one for the doctor's visit and for medication given to the decedent during the visit. The medication notice will let you know if the doctor administered drug is approved or denied.

Even though payment is not requested, it is important to verify that the bill is valid for two reasons:

➢ LATER LIABILITY

If the insurer refuses to pay the claim, the facility will seek payment from whoever is in possession of the decedent's property, and that may reduce the amount inherited by the beneficiaries.

➢ INCREASED HEALTH CARE COSTS

Regardless of whether the decedent was covered by a private health care insurer or Medicare, improper billing increases the cost of health insurance to all of us. Consumers pay high premiums for health coverage. We, as taxpayers, all share the cost of Medicare. We all pay, if unnecessary or fraudulent billing is not checked. If you believe that you have come across a case of Medicare fraud, call the ANTI-FRAUD HOT-LINE at (800) 447-8477 and report the incident to the Office of the Inspector General of the United States Department of Health and Human Services.

HOW TO CHECK MEDICARE BILLING

The structure of Medicare has changed giving people the option of staying with the *Original Medicare Plan* or choosing a *Medicare Advantage Plan* such as a Medicare Health Maintenance Organization ("HMO"), or other Medicare Health Plans. Coverage depends on which plan is chosen. You need to determine whether the decedent was covered under the Original Medicare Plan, or some other Medicare Plan. The publication *Medicare and You* explains coverage under the different options. See page 52 of this book, to obtain a copy of the booklet. Coverage under any of the other plans is explained in the membership materials given to the decedent at the time he signed up for the plan.

BILLING UNDER THE ORIGINAL MEDICARE PLAN

ASSIGNMENT

An important billing question for those under the Original Medicare Plan is whether the health care provider agreed to accept Medicare *assignment*, meaning that they agreed to accept the Medicare-approved amount. If so, the patient is responsible to pay any Medicare deductible and coinsurance amounts (usually 20% of the approved amount).

Doctors and health care providers who do not accept assignment, are limited in the amount they can charge for a Medicare covered service. The highest they can charge is **15%** over the Medicare-approved amount. This *Limiting Charge* applies only to certain services and does not apply to supplies and equipment. For more information about assignment you can call (800) 633-4227 for your free copy of *Does your doctor or supplier accept "assignment?"* or you can down-load the publication from the Medicare Website.
http://www.medicare.gov

ADVANCE BENEFICIARY NOTICE

For those who are in the Original Medicare Plan, a doctor or a supplier may give notice saying that Medicare probably will not pay for the service that is about to be provided. This is called an **Advance Beneficiary Notice**.

Other Medicare Plans also notify the patient in the event that the service is not covered under the plan. If the patient still wants the service after receiving such notice, he will be asked to sign an agreement stating that he will pay for the service in the event that Medicare does not pay.

If all of this appears confusing, it is.

To check the decedent's Medicare billing, you need the answers to the following questions:

What is the plan?

Determine whether the decedent was in the Original Medicare Plan or some other Medicare Health Plan.

What is covered under the plan?

The *Medicare and You* booklet explains what is covered under the Original Medicare Plan. You will need a copy of the membership materials for the Medicare Advantage Plans to determine what is covered under that plan.

Does the Provider accept Assignment?

If the decedent was in the Original Medicare Plan, you need to determine whether the health care provider accepted assignment; and if not, whether the Limiting Charge applies to the services provided. If assignment is accepted, or the Limiting Charge applies, you need to determine the Medicare-approved amount.

Did the decedent agree to pay?

Check to see whether the decedent was given notice that the service would not be covered by Medicare; and if so, whether he signed a contract agreeing to pay in the event that Medicare refuses to pay.

Did the decedent have a Medigap Policy?

A **Medigap Policy** is a health insurance policy sold by private insurance in accordance with state and federal law. It is Medicare Supplemental Insurance. If the decedent had a Medigap Policy, get a copy of the contract and see if the goods or services provided are covered under the Policy.

DENIAL OF MEDICARE COVERAGE

If the health care provider reports to you that a service provided to the decedent is not covered by Medicare, or if the facility submits the bill and Medicare refuses to pay, check to see if you agree with that ruling by getting answers to the questions on the prior page. You can appeal that decision if you believe that the decedent was wrongly denied coverage.

If the decedent was in the Original Medicare Plan, you will find information about how to file an appeal on the Medicare Summary Notice. If he opted for a Medicare Advantage Plan or some other Medicare Health Plan, you will find that information in his health care plan materials. The book *Your Medicare Rights and Protections* (CMS Pub. No. 10112) contains information about appeals. You can get a free copy by calling (800) 633-4227 or by down-loading it from the Medicare Website. http://www.medicare.gov.

The U.S. Department of Health and Human Services is in charge of Medicare Appeals. They hold hearings with video conference equipment or by telephone. They allow you to appeal in person before an Administrative Law Judge only if "special or extraordinary circumstances exist."

Even if an in-person hearing is allowed, a hearing before an Administrative Law Judge is currently available in only four locations: Miami, Florida; Cleveland, Ohio; Irvine, California and Arlington, Virginia. Those who insist on a face-to-face hearing lose their right to receive a decision within 90 days, so it may take considerable time before the matter is settled.

GETTING HELP WITH THE APPEAL

You can appeal the decision yourself, but it is best to first call the Arizona Department of Economic Security, Aging and Adult Administration to learn how to present your case (ARS 46-452.01). Within Arizona, you can call toll free (800) 852-5494. Out of state call (602) 542-4446.

If you want an attorney to help with your appeal, call the State Bar of Arizona Lawyer Referral Service at (602) 340-7300 for a referral to an attorney experienced in Medicare appeals. Some attorneys work *pro bono* (literally for the public good; i.e. without charge) but most charge to assist in an appeal.

Federal statute 42 U.S.C. 406(a)(2)(A) limits the amount an attorney may charge for a successful Medicare appeal to 25% of the amount recovered or $4,000, whichever is the smaller amount.

Medicaid is a program that provides medical and long term nursing care for people with low income and limited resources. The program is funded jointly by the federal and state government. Federal law requires the state to recover monies spent from the Estate of a Medicaid recipient who was 55 or older when the decedent received Medicaid assistance. The state will seek reimbursement for the cost of nursing home care or for home based care or other community based services (42 U.S.C. 1396(p)).

There usually is no money to recover because to qualify for Medicaid in Arizona, a person may not have more than $2,000 in assets. But sometimes it happens that a person on Medicaid dies and his Estate later receives money perhaps as part of a settlement of a lawsuit. Also, it could happen that he owned a home in his name only. Owning a home does not disqualify a person from receiving Medicaid, however if he received institutional care Medicaid benefits after age 55, the state has the right to place a lien on that home and seek recovery from the proceeds of the sale of the house. In Arizona, a lien cannot be placed against the home if the patient's spouse, minor or disabled child, or if a sibling has co-owned the home for more than an year (ARS 36-2935).

The Personal Representative needs to notify the state that they have a right to file a claim against the Estate to recover monies spent for the benefit of the decedent. He can call the decedent's caseworker or Arizona's Health Care Cost Containment System at (602) 417-4000 for information about where to send notice.

SOME THINGS ARE CREDITOR PROOF

Sometimes it happens that the decedent had money or property titled in his name only, but he also had a significant amount of debt. In such cases the beneficiaries may wonder whether they should go through a Probate procedure if there will be little, if anything, left after the creditors are paid. Before making the decision consider that some assets are protected under Arizona law:

✧ LIFE INSURANCE PROCEEDS ✧

Life insurance proceeds paid to a beneficiary as a result of the decedent's death are exempt from the claims of the decedent's creditors; however if the proceeds of the policy are payable to the decedent or to his Estate, those proceeds become part of his Probate Estate and are available to pay his debts.

If the surviving spouse is the beneficiary of the insurance policy, he/she may be equally responsible for monies owed by the decedent. Under Arizona law, $20,000 of the proceeds of an insurance policy on the decedent's life, that is payable to the surviving spouse, is free from the claims of the decedent's creditors and the creditors of the surviving spouse, as well (ARS 20-1131, 33-1126).

✧ FEDERAL RETIREMENT PLANS ✧

Federal retirement plans 401(a), 403 a & b, 408 A, 409, and deferred plans under section 457 of the US Internal Revenue Code are exempt from the claims of creditors. All monies received by beneficiaries of these plans are protected from the creditors of the decedent. The only exception is monies he owed for back child support by order of a Court (ARS 33-1126C).

PROTECTION FOR THE SURVIVING SPOUSE

✧ THE HOMESTEAD ALLOWANCE ✧

The surviving spouse is entitled to keep $18,000 exempt from the claims of creditors. This amount is called the *Homestead Allowance*. If the decedent was single with minor or dependent children, they are entitled to divide the $18,000 between them (ARS 14-2402).

✧ THE FAMILY ALLOWANCE ✧

The surviving spouse and dependent children are entitled to a reasonable allowance for their maintenance while the Probate procedure is being conducted. This *Family Allowance* can be paid in a lump sum, or monthly, but the total amount cannot exceed $12,000 without a special order from the court (ARS 14-2404, 14-2405). The Family Allowance is exempt from the claims of creditors.

✧ EXEMPT PROPERTY ✧

In addition to the Family Allowance, the surviving spouse is entitled to keep any of the following items:

household furniture; automobiles
furnishings; appliances; personal effects

up to $7,000 in value (not counting monies owed on the property). If the value of these items does not add up to $7,000, the spouse is entitled to any other asset of the decedent's Estate to make up the $7,000 value. If the decedent was single, his children are entitled to divide the *exempt property* equally among themselves (ARS 14-2403).

✧ THE HOMESTEAD EXEMPTION ✧

Anyone who resides in the state of Arizona is entitled to a *Homestead Exemption* in the amount of $150,000 of equity in the property. By *equity* we mean the current value of the property, less monies owed on it. If a person owns their residence, a creditor cannot force the sale of the property unless there is more than $150,000 in equity in the homestead. The Homestead Exemption does not apply to someone who holds a mortgage on the property or for labor or construction liens on the property (ARS 33-1103).

Only one Homestead Exemption may be claimed by a married couple, but if the decedent owned the homestead jointly with his spouse, Homestead Exemption now belongs to his spouse. If he was single, the exemption is lost once he dies (ARS 33-1101).

✧ OUT OF STATE INCOME TAX ✧

If the decedent retired to Arizona and was receiving a pension check, or monies from a retirement plan from another state, those pension funds are protected by Arizona law from any income tax that the other state might levy against those funds. The other state can get a judgment for taxes owed in that state on pension funds that the decedent received while in Arizona, but they will not be able to collect on it (ARS 33-1151),

This protection extends to the surviving spouse and dependent children. If the spouse, or dependent children, inherit all of the decedent's property, the other state will not be able to collect their income tax from that inheritance. This protection does not extend to anyone else. If the decedent was single and without a dependent child, the out of state income tax can be collected from the Probate Estate.

Next, consider that not all Probate debts are equal. If there are insufficient funds in the Probate Estate to pay for all claims against the decedent's Estate, then Arizona Statute (ARS 14-3805) establishes an order of priority for payment:

CLASS 1: COST AND EXPENSES OF ADMINISTRATION

The cost of the Probate procedure, including filing fees, and fees charged by the Personal Representative and his attorney, must be satisfied before any other debt can be paid.

PROVISION FOR THE FAMILY

Once the cost of the administration is paid, the Probate Court can award the Homestead Allowance, the Family Allowance and the Exempt Property to the surviving spouse and/or children (ARS 14-2404, 14-2405).

CLASS 2: REASONABLE FUNERAL EXPENSES

The reasonable expenses of the decedent's funeral and burial are second in priority.

CLASS 3: FEDERAL TAXES

Debts or taxes owed by the decedent to the federal government are third in line for payment.

CLASS 4: MEDICAL EXPENSES

Fourth in line is payment for the reasonable and necessary medical expenses of the decedent's last illness, including payment to those who provided nursing or custodial care.

CLASS 5: STATE TAXES

Debts or taxes owed by the decedent to the state of Arizona are a Class 5 debt.

CLASS 6: ALL OTHER CLAIMS

There are no priorities within a given class. For example, suppose the decedent left enough money to pay for the his funeral and the Probate procedure, with $20,000 left over. If there are no other debts, his beneficiaries will inherit the $20,000 (ARS 14-3805).

Suppose instead that he left a hospital bill of $30,000 and a doctor's bill of $10,000 (both Class 4 debts). The $20,000 will be prorated with the hospital getting $15,000 and the doctor getting $5,000. There will be nothing left to pay any other claim. There will be nothing left for anyone to inherit.

✧ THERE IS A STATUTE OF LIMITATIONS ✧

There are federal and state laws that set time periods for pursuing a claim. Anyone who wishes to take court action must do so within the time set by the given Statute of Limitation. For example, a law suit for the wrongful death of the decedent must be filed within two years of the death (ARS 12-542).

There is a Statute of Limitations for a creditor to come forward and make a claim against the decedent's Estate for monies owed. The Personal Representative is required to publish notice of the death in a newspaper of general circulation for three successive weeks. The creditor has four months from the first day that notice was published to file a claim with the Probate Court (ARS 14-3801).

But what if no one starts a Probate procedure? Arizona statute 14-3803 imposes a two year Statute of Limitations from the date of the decedent's death. If a claim is not filed within two years after the death, that claim cannot be enforced against the Estate, the Personal Representative, or any of the beneficiaries.

There are exceptions to the two-year limit such as mortgages and federal claims and certain liens on the decedent's property. But, in general, if no one starts a Probate procedure and two years have passed from the date of the death, the beneficiaries may be able to obtain possession of the decedent's assets free from creditor claims.

Some may be thinking it is a good idea to postpone Probate until two years have passed.

Read on before you decide to wait out the two years.

 **LAWYER** DECENT LEAVING
CONSIDERABLE DEBT

If the decedent died leaving much debt and no property, the solution is simple. No Probate, no one gets paid. But if the decedent had property and died owing more money than the property was worth, his heirs may decide that going through Probate is just not worth the effort, or they may decide to simply wait out the two year Statute of Limitation period and begin Probate at that time.

This may not be the best decision. Some creditors are tenacious and will use whatever legal strategy is available in order to be paid, including initiating the Probate procedure themselves. If no one else files for Probate within 45 days from the date of death, a creditor can petition the Court to be appointed Personal Representative of the Estate (ARS 14-3203).

As we will see in Chapter 6 , a Personal Representative has much authority when conducting the Probate procedure. Family members may object to having a creditor as a Personal Representative, so there could be a court battle over who has priority to be appointed as Personal Representative. Court battles are expensive, emotionally as well as financially. Before you decide to distance yourself from the Probate procedure, consult with an attorney experienced in Probate matters for an opinion about the best way to administer the Estate.

Suppose you owed money to the decedent. Do you need to pay that debt now that he is dead? That depends on whether there is some written document that says the debt is forgiven once the decedent dies. For example, suppose the decedent loaned you money to buy your home. If he left a Will saying that once he dies, your debt is forgiven, then you do not need to make any more payments. If you signed a promissory note and mortgage at the time you borrowed the money from the decedent, the Personal Representative should sign the original promissory note **PAID IN FULL** and return the note to you. If the mortgage was recorded, the Personal Representative needs to have a Satisfaction of Mortgage recorded in the county where the property is located. You should receive the recorded Satisfaction for your records.

If you owed the decedent money and there is no Will, or if there is a Will, and no mention of forgiving the debt, then you still owe the money. Money borrowed from the decedent and his spouse needs to be repaid to the spouse. Money borrowed from the decedent only, becomes an asset of the Estate of the decedent, meaning that you owe the money to the decedent's Estate. If you are one of the beneficiaries of the Estate, you may be able to deduct the money from your inheritance.

For example, suppose your father left $80,000 to be divided equally between you and your brother. If you owed your father $20,000, your father's Estate is really worth $100,000, with each child entitled to $50,000. Instead of paying the $20,000, you can agree to receive $30,000 and have the $20,000 debt forgiven. Your brother will receive the remaining $50,000.

Who Are The Beneficiaries? 5

A question that comes up early on is who is entitled to the property of the decedent. To answer the question you first need to know how the property was titled (owned) as of the date of death.

There are three ways to own property. The decedent could have owned property jointly with another person, or in trust for another person; or the decedent could have owned property that was titled in his name only.

In general, upon the decedent's death:

> **Joint Property With Right of Survivorship**
> belongs to the surviving joint owner.
>
> **Trust Property** belongs to the beneficiary
> of the Trust.
>
> Property owned by the **decedent only** is inherited
> by the beneficiaries named in the Will.
> If there is no Will, the property goes to his heirs
> according to Arizona's Laws of Intestate Succession.
>
> **NOTE** ⇨ If the decedent was married, his
> spouse may have rights in his property.

This chapter describes each type of ownership in detail.

PROPERTY OWNED JOINTLY

Bank accounts, securities, motor vehicles, real property can all be owned jointly by two or more people. If one of the joint owners dies, then the survivor(s) continue to own their share of the property. Who owns the share belonging to the decedent depends on how the joint ownership was set up.

THE JOINT BANK ACCOUNT

When a bank account is opened the depositors sign an agreement with the bank that states the terms and conditions of the account. If two or more people open a bank account, it is referred to as a *Joint* or *Multiple Party Account*. During their lifetime, each person named the account is entitled to as much as they contributed unless there is clear evidence of a different intent. If a husband and wife own the account, it is presumed they each own half of the account (ARS 14-6211).

When a joint account is opened the parties sign a contract of deposit with the bank saying who will get their share of the account should one of them die. If they do not want the joint owner of the account to inherit the other's share of the account, the contract of deposit with the bank will state:
"At death of party, deceased party's ownership
passes as part of deceased party's Estate"
or the contract of deposit will identify the account as a
Tenancy In Common.
In these cases, there is no *right of survivorship*. If one owner dies, his share of the account will go the beneficiaries named in his Will. If there is no Will, the decedent's share goes to his heirs as determined by Arizona's Laws of Intestate Succession. These Laws are explained later in this Chapter.

Once an owner of a joint account with right of survivorship dies, the surviving owner is free to withdraw all of the monies from the account without the need to go through Probate; but understanding that he may be responsible to pay Estate or Succession Taxes on money he inherits from the account; and also understanding that if there is a Probate procedure the Personal Representative has the right to ask the surviving joint owner to contribute as much from the decedent's share of the account as is necessary to settle the decedent's Estate (ARS 14-6215).

If there is no right of survivorship, upon notice of the death, the bank will freeze the account until the beneficiaries of the decedent's share of the account can be determined. If a surviving owner withdraws all of the money from the account either just before, or after death, he may be liable to the decedent's Estate for monies improperly withdrawn.

If a joint account is set up with right of survivorship, and there are three owners, should one die, the survivors own the account. How much of the account is owned by each surviving owner is determined by Arizona law. Specifically, if the deceased owner's spouse was a joint owner of the account, the spouse is entitled to the decedent's share of the account. If the decedent was not married to either of the joint owners, his net contribution to the account (i.e., how much he contributed, less how much he withdrew) is divided equally between the surviving owners.

For example, suppose a husband, wife, and son own a bank account, should the wife die, the husband owns the wife's share of the account, but if the son dies first, his share will be divided equally between his parent (ARS 14-6212).

JOINTLY HELD SECURITIES

You can determine whether the decedent owns a security alone or jointly with another by examining the face of the stock or bond certificate. If two names are printed on the certificate followed by a statement that the owners are "Joint Tenants With Right of Survivorship ("JTWRS")," the surviving owner can either cash in the security or ask the company to issue a new certificate in the name of the surviving owner.

Each state has its own securities regulations. If the security was issued in another state, how the account was set up will determine who will inherit the property once the owner dies (ARS 14-6303). If a security held in two or more names, was registered or purchased in another state, and it does not indicate whether there is a right of survivorship, you need to contact the company to determine how the account was set up; i.e. with or without survivorship rights.

If the decedent held his securities in a brokerage account, you need to check the monthly or quarterly brokerage statement to see if the account was owned jointly. Not all brokerage firms print the name of a joint owner on the brokerage statement, so you need to contact the firm to determine whether there is a surviving joint owner, or perhaps a beneficiary of the account.

Request a copy of the contract that is the basis of the account. The contract will show the terms of the brokerage account and when it was opened.

If a motor vehicle or a boat is owned jointly, the name of the owners are printed on the certificate of title. Joint ownership is indicated by the words "AND" or "OR" or "AND/OR" for example, the title can be:

HENRY LEE OR DAVID LEE

HENRY LEE AND DAVID LEE

HENRY LEE AND/OR DAVID LEE.

Each of these designations has a different meaning.

AND "AND" means that both signatures are required to transfer title. Should one owner die, the Personal Representative will need to transfer the decedent's "half" of the car to the proper beneficiary. Transferring title is explained in Chapter 6.

OR "OR" means that during their lifetime either is free to transfer title on his signature alone.

AND/OR "AND/OR" means that there is a Right of Survivorship. During the lifetime of the parties, both signatures are required to transfer title to the vehicle, however, should one die the survivor owns the car.

It is important to change title as soon as you are able. You might be able to get a reduced insurance rate if there is only one person insured under the policy. Also, should the surviving owner be involved in an accident, and title has officially been changed, there is no question that the Estate of the decedent is in any way liable for the accident.

REAL PROPERTY OWNED JOINTLY

The name of the owner of real property is printed on the face of the deed. To determine whether the decedent owned the property jointly with another person, you need to look at the last recorded deed. The deed will indicate joint ownership. For example:

> For the consideration of $200,000,
> I, WILLIAM TRAYNOR, a single man,
> hereby convey to
> RICHARD CODY, a single man
> and HENRY CODY, a married man, as
> **JOINT TENANTS WITH RIGHT OF SURVIVORSHIP**
> all that real property situated in
> the county of Pima, state of Arizona
> with legal description . . .

William is the *Grantor* of the deed. That means he transferred the property to Richard and Henry Cody who are the *Grantees* and present owners of the property. The deed states that Richard and Henry are JOINT TENANTS WITH RIGHT OF SURVIVORSHIP. Should one of them die, the surviving joint tenant will own the property 100%. Nothing need be done to establish the ownership, however the decedent's name remains on the deed.

If you are the surviving joint owner of real property, you want to file an AFFIDAVIT OF SURVIVING JOINT TENANT with the County Recorder to let everyone know that you are now the sole owner of the property. See Chapter 6 for an explanation of the transfer of real property.

🗐 DEED HELD AS TENANT IN COMMON

If a deed identifies the decedent and another as TENANTS IN COMMON, the decedent's share belongs to whomever he named as his beneficiary in his Will. If he died without a Will, Arizona's Laws of Intestate Succession determine who inherits the decedent's share of the property. A Probate procedure will be necessary to transfer the decedent's share of the property to the proper beneficiary.

In Arizona, there is no implied Right of Survivorship. If the deed names two or more people as the Grantee but does not identify whether they are Tenants In Common or Joint Tenants With Right of Survivorship, they own the property as Tenants in Common.

There are exceptions to the rule. If an owner of real property transfers the property to himself and someone else without stating whether there is a right of survivorship, then a Joint Tenancy With Right of Survivorship is created. For example, if RICHARD GOMEZ conveys to
RICHARD GOMEZ and his brother JOSE GOMEZ
should either brother die, the property will belong to the surviving owner. Similarly, if a married couple hold title as Community Property, they can create a right of survivorship by transferring the property to themselves as husband and wife (ARS 33-431).

There are other exceptions to the rule, so if there are two or more Grantees and the deed does not clearly identify them as Tenants In Common or Joint Tenants With Right of Survivorship, then it is important to consult with an experienced Probate attorney to determine who owns the property should one of the owners die.

🗎 DEED HELD AS HUSBAND AND WIFE

In many states, a deed held as husband and wife means that the surviving partner owns the property. This is not the case in Arizona. It is presumed that real property held as husband and wife is Community Property with each partner owning half. If the decedent and his spouse owned real property as:

HUSBAND AND WIFE AS COMMUNITY PROPERTY

this is the same as a Tenancy In Common. The decedent's "half" will go to whoever is named in the decedent's Will, or if no Will according to the Laws of Intestate Succession. But if the decedent owned property with his spouse as:

JOINT TENANTS WITH RIGHT OF SURVIVORSHIP

the property now belongs to the surviving spouse.

Similarly, if the decedent owned property with his spouse as COMMUNITY PROPERTY WITH RIGHT OF SURVIVORSHIP the property is owned 100% by the surviving spouse.

Either party of property held as Community Property With Right of Survivorship can, without the permission of the other, withdraw the right of survivorship by signing an AFFIDAVIT TERMINATING RIGHT OF SURVIVORSHIP and recording the Affidavit in the office of the Recorder in the county where the property is located (ARS 33-431).

If the deed is a Community Property deed with right of survivorship, it is important to have an attorney or a title company do a title search to be sure that such Affidavit was not filed.

▤ THE BENEFICIARY DEED

The BENEFICIARY DEED is a relatively new form of deed. It enables property to be transferred to a beneficiary without going through a Probate proceeding, with the added advantage of giving the owner of the property complete control of the property during his lifetime. For example, a husband and wife can sign a Beneficiary Deed giving the property to their son once they are both deceased:

> We, ELENA RAMOS and PETER RAMOS,
> Joint Tenants With Right of Survivorship
> hereby convey to EDWARD RAMOS
> **EFFECTIVE ON OUR DEATH,**
> the following described real property
>
> . . .

The Grantee (Edward) has no right to the property while his parents are alive. Once both Elena and Peter are deceased, Ralph will own the property without the need for any Probate procedure.

During their lifetime, his parents are free to sell the property without notifying Edward that they are doing so. They are free to take back the gift by revoking the deed. Revoking the deed is simple. All they need do is file a REVOCATION OF BENEFICIARY DEED with the County Recorder in the county where the property is located. Both joint owners must sign the revocation for it to be effective; but if one owner is deceased, the surviving owner, can revoke the deed on his own signature (ARS 33-405).

🖩 DEED WITH A LIFE ESTATE

A *Life Estate* interest in real property means that the person who owns the Life Estate has the right to live in that property until he dies. You can identify a Life Estate interest by examining the face of the deed. If somewhere on the face of the deed you see the phrase RESERVING A LIFE ESTATE to the deceased Grantor, then the Grantee now owns the property. For example, suppose the granting paragraph of the deed reads:

> LEONA CAVALLO, a single woman for value received, hereby grants to FRANK CAVALLO, a married man, the following described real property
>
> . . .
>
> RESERVING A LIFE ESTATE
> TO ROSE CAVALLO
>
> . . .

Leona is the owner of the Life Estate. Frank owns the *Remainder Interest* in the property. Frank has no right to occupy the property during Leona's lifetime, but once she dies, he will own the property 100%. He will be free to take possession of the property or transfer it, as he sees fit. As with a survivorship tenancy, nothing need be done to establish Frank's ownership of the property, however, see Chapter 6 for information about documents that can be recorded to notify anyone examining title to the property that Frank now owns the property.

 **LAWYER**   THE OUT OF STATE DEED

The laws of the state or country where the property is located determine who inherits property in that state. If the decedent owned property in another state or country, then even if the decedent was a resident of Arizona, the laws of the state where the property is located determine who inherits property in that state.

The laws of each state are similar, but not the same. Some states, do not require the deed to specifically say there is a right of survivorship. In such states, a deed held as Joint Tenants means that there is a right of survivorship, even if the deed does not say so. Other states are like Arizona, requiring that the deed state there is a right of survivorship. If not, the property is owned as a Tenancy In Common. Rights of married couples varies significantly state to state. In some states, survivorship rights are created if married couple own the property as "Husband and Wife" or as "Tenants By The Entirety."

If the decedent owned property in another state, it is important to consult with an attorney in that state to determine who now owns the property.

   THERE COULD BE A LATER DEED

The above discussion on the different types of ownership of real property assumes that you are in possession of the most recent, valid deed. The decedent could have signed another, later deed. Before you come to a conclusion about who inherits the property it is advisable to have a title search by an attorney or a title insurance company to determine the owner of the property as of the decedent's date of death.

PROPERTY HELD IN TRUST

BANK/ SECURITY ACCOUNTS

A bank account or security account that is registered in the name of the decedent "In Trust For" or "for the benefit of" someone, will be turned over to the beneficiary once the financial institution has a certified copy of the death certificate. If the beneficiary is a minor, and the account balance is under $10,000, the company may give the money to a Trust company or an adult who is caring for the child; but if it is over that amount, the company will not transfer the funds without permission from the Probate Court (ARS 14-7657). Some companies will seek Court approval even if the sum is less than $10,000. See Chapter 7 for a discussion of transfers made to minors.

BANK ACCOUNT HELD BY A TRUSTEE

If the bank or security account is registered in the name of the decedent "as Trustee under a Trust Agreement," that means the decedent was the Trustee of a Trust and the bank will turn over that account to the Successor Trustee of the Trust. Banks usually require a copy of the Trust Agreement or an affidavit that identifies the Successor Trustee, so the bank should be aware of his identity. If the Trust was amended to name a different Successor Trustee, you need to present the bank with a copy of that amendment together with a certified copy of the death certificate.

MOTOR VEHICLE

If the motor vehicle is held in the name of the decedent "as Trustee," then the motor vehicle continues to be Trust property. The Successor Trustee will need to contact the Motor Vehicle Division to have title changed to that of the Successor Trustee. The Successor Trustee will then dispose of the car according to the terms of the Trust Agreement.

REAL PROPERTY

If the decedent had a Trust and put real property that he owned into the Trust, then the deed may read something like this:

> JOHN ZAMORA and MARIA ZAMORA, his wife,
> of Maricopa County, Arizona
> for consideration paid, grants to
> JOHN ZAMORA, **Trustee,**
> **or his successors in Trust, under the**
> **JOHN ZAMORA REVOCABLE TRUST AGREEMENT**
> DATED JANUARY 2, 2006
> the following described real property
> . . .

The death of the Trustee of a Trust does not change the ownership of the property. It remains in the Trust. The Trust document might say whether the person who takes John's place as Trustee (the Successor Trustee) should sell or keep the property or perhaps give it to a beneficiary. If no instruction is given, the Successor Trustee can use his discretion as to what to do with the property. If you are a beneficiary of the Trust and are concerned about what the Successor Trustee will do with the property, then it is best to consult with your attorney to learn about your rights under that Trust.

A DEED OF TRUST

A Trust Deed is very different from the above described deed. The Trust Deed is essentially a mortgage. The owner of the property places title to the property with a Trustee as security for payment of monies owed to the lender. If the debt is not paid, the Trustee (after proper foreclosure on the property) will deliver title to the property to the Beneficiary of the Trust Deed, namely the lender.

If the decedent owned property that was in his name only (not jointly or in trust for someone), some sort of Probate procedure will be necessary in order to transfer the property to the proper beneficiary. Who is entitled to the decedent's Probate Estate depends on whether he died with or without a valid Will. If the decedent died *testate* (with a valid Will), the beneficiaries of the decedent's property are identified in his Will.

If the decedent died without a valid Will, i.e., intestate, the Arizona Laws of Intestate Succession determine who inherits the decedent's Probate Estate and what percentage of the Estate each heir is to receive once the bills and costs of administering the Estate are paid.

Arizona's Law of Intestate Succession recognizes the right of the family to inherit the decedent's property. The law covers all possible relationships beginning with the decedent's spouse. But before discussing the rights of the surviving spouse we need to consider whether the decedent had a marriage that is considered to be valid in the state of Arizona.

To be married in Arizona means that a man and a woman have obtained a license to marry from the state, solemnized the marriage by a state or religious ceremony, and then cohabited together as man and wife. Parental consent to marry is required for anyone under 18. If the person is under 16, parental consent and permission from a Superior Court judge is required (ARS 25-102).

☒ BIGAMY

It is against the law for a married person to marry. No license can be granted if one of the parties is currently married; with the exception of someone whose spouse has been missing for five consecutive years, and whose absence is unexplained, even though there has been a diligent search (ARS 14-1107).

Arizona law specifically prohibits the marriage of people

☒ who are *ancestors* (parent, grandparents, etc.)
or *descendants* (child, grandchild, etc.)
of each other

☒ who are aunt and nephew or uncle and niece

☒ who are brother and sister. This includes siblings who are half blood; i.e. they have only one parent in common.

Marriage between first cousins is prohibited with the exception of those cousins who are 65 years of age or older. First cousins who are younger than 65 may marry with the approval of a Superior Court judge. To get his approval, they will need to prove that at least one of the couple is unable to reproduce (ARS 25-101).

☒ SAME SEX

In 1998, the federal government passed the Defense Marriage Act, saying that for purposes of federal law, marriage is a legal union between one man and one woman (28 U.S.C. 1738C). However, for purposes of state law, whether you can marry, who you can marry; and how you can marry, are determined by the laws of the state in which you live. There is much variation state to state. Vermont and Connecticut have approved same-sex *Civil Unions*. Massachusetts allows gay marriages.

The Defense of Marriage Act also provides that no state is required to recognize the laws of another state as relating to same sex marriage. And this is the case in Arizona. Arizona law bans same sex marriages and will not recognize a marriage between those of the same gender regardless of whether that relationship is legal anywhere else (ARS 25-101).

Some states, such as California, ban same sex marriages, yet Domestic Partners who are registered with the state have all of the rights and responsibilities allowed to a married couple within the state. Some states such as Florida and New York do not have a state registry for Domestic Partner, but certain local or county governments have a registry giving Domestic Partners certain rights such as the right to visit each other in hospitals or jail, decide on the partners funeral arrangements, participate in the partner's health plan, etc.

It is important to consult with an attorney if you have any question about the validity of the decedent's marriage.

THE COMMON LAW MARRIAGE

A Common Law marriage is one that has not been solemnized by ceremony. It is more than just living together. The couple agree to live together as man and wife, and then publicly hold themselves out as being married. Many states, including Arizona, do not recognize a Common Law marriage as being valid. But Arizona respects the laws of other states, and will recognize a Common Law marriage if it is valid in the state where the couple entered into the marriage; provided such marriages are not prohibited under Arizona law (bigamous, incestuous, or same sex marriages) (ARS 25-112).

THE COVENANT MARRIAGE

Due to concerns regarding high divorce rates and the dissolution of the "traditional family unit," the Arizona legislature created a **Covenant Marriage.** The Covenant Marriage is essentially a reinforcement of the "till death do us part." To receive a Covenant Marriage certificate, the couple must covenant (promise) that they will agree to get counseling before filing for divorce; and that they do not intend to divorce except on certain grounds, which are basically the same "fault" grounds in previous divorce laws (drug abuse, adultery, abandonment, etc.).

The Covenant Marriage and the non-Covenant Marriage have significant differences should the parties decide to separate during their lifetime, however there are no differences when it comes to the Laws of Intestate Succession. Either way the couple is considered to be married in the state of Arizona, with the full rights and responsibilities of a married couple. Should one of the partners die without a Will, the surviving spouse is entitled to inherit the decedent's property according to Arizona's Laws of Intestate Succession (ARS 25-901, 25-903).

If the decedent died without a valid Will, the state of Arizona provides one for him in the form of its *Laws of Intestate Succession*. Arizona is a Community Property state so if the decedent was married the Laws of Intestate Succession apply to:

⇨ all of his Separate Property, and

⇨ half of the couple's Community Property.

We will refer to property inherited according to the Laws of Intestate Succession as the decedent's **Intestate Estate**.

SINGLE WITH DESCENDANTS

If the decedent was not married when he died, but he had descendants, then they inherit all of his property **by representation**. Arizona statute 14-2709 (A) defines "by representation" as follows:

> If an applicable statute or a governing instrument calls for property to be distributed **by representation** or **per capita at each generation**, the property is divided into as many equal shares as there are surviving descendants in the generation nearest to the designated ancestor that contains one or more surviving descendants and deceased descendants in the same generation who left any surviving descendants. Each surviving descendant in the nearest generation is allocated one share. Any remaining shares are combined and then divided in the same manner among the surviving descendants of the deceased descendants as if the surviving descendants who were allocated a share and their surviving descendants had predeceased the distribution date.

If you understood the above definition and you are not a lawyer, then you missed your calling. For the rest of us (even lawyers) its a head-scratcher. Perhaps the best way to explain the term is through example.

ALL CHILDREN SURVIVE

Suppose the decedent was single and had four children, Ann, Barry, Carl, David. If he dies without a Will, each child will get 25% of his Estate.

CHILD WITHOUT DESCENDANTS DIES BEFORE DECEDENT

If Ann dies before her father leaving no descendants, Barry, Carl and David divide the Estate between them. Each gets one third of the Estate.

CHILDREN WITH DESCENDANTS DIES BEFORE DECEDENT

Suppose instead that only Carl and David survived their father. If Ann died leaving 2 children and Barry died leaving 3 children, the Estate is divided into 4 shares — one for each surviving child and one share for each deceased child who left descendants.

Carl and David each get their 25% share. The remaining 50% of the estate is divided equally among the five grand-children; i.e., each gets 10% of the Estate.

✧ MARRIED

If the decedent was married with no surviving descendant, or if all of his children are also those of the surviving spouse, all of the Intestate Estate goes to the surviving spouse. If the decedent was married, but not all of his children are those of the surviving spouse, the spouse is entitled to half of the decedent's Separate Property. His children inherit the other half of his Separate Property and his share of the Community Property, by representation (ARS 14-2102).

✧ SINGLE, NO DESCENDANT

If the decedent was single, without descendants, his parents share equally in his Estate. If he is survived by one parent only, that parent inherits all of his Intestate Estate. If neither parent survives him, the Estate is inherited by the descendants of his parents; i.e., the decedent's brothers and sisters, or the nieces and nephews of a deceased sibling (ARS 14-2103 (3)). The property is distributed "by representation at each generation," meaning that the shares are distributed among the nieces and nephews in the same manner as explained in the example given on the previous page.

HALF BLOOD INHERITS THE SAME AS WHOLE BLOOD

A relative who is related by half blood inherits the same as one who is related by whole blood (ARS 14-2107). For example, if the decedent had a brother with the same parent and two sisters with the same father but a different mother, all three siblings are entitled to an equal share of the decedent's Intestate Estate.

✧ SINGLE, NO DESCENDANT, NO PARENT, NO SIBLING

If the decedent was single, without descendants, parents, or their descendants, the Estate is divided in half with one share going to his maternal grandparents, in equal shares. If they are deceased, the share goes to their descendants, i.e., the decedent's aunts and uncles or their descendants, by representation. The other half is distributed to the decedent's paternal grandparents in the same manner. If there are no relatives on the maternal side, all of the Estate goes to his paternal relative, and vis versa (ARS 14-2103 (4)).

We could give you an example of how the Estate is distributed if the decedent is survived only by descendants of his grandparents, but we thought you might enjoy a puzzle instead:

Winston died intestate leaving $100,000. His only relatives are his mother's sister, Aunt Susie, and her children, Ramona and Abigail and a first cousin Elvis, on his father's side. How much does each relative receive?

You can check your answer by visiting the puzzle section of the Eagle Publishing Company Website.
http://www.eaglepublishing.com

ARIZONA: HEIR OF LAST RESORT
Property that is either unclaimed or abandoned, goes to the state, so if the decedent died with absolutely no next of kin, the state of Arizona "inherits" the Intestate Estate (ARS 14-2105).

CAUTION   IT ISN'T ALL THAT SIMPLE

The discussion of Arizona's Laws of Intestate Succession is abridged. There is much more to the law. For example, anyone who inherits property under the Laws of Intestate Succession must survive the decedent by at least 120 hours (5 days); and if not, that share is distributed as if that person died before the decedent. This rule is not applied if to do so will result in the state of Arizona inheriting the property (ARS 14-2104).

Unless the descent is straight forward, with the decedent leaving a surviving spouse and/or children (all who survive him), it is best to consult with an attorney before you decide who is entitled to inherit the decedent's Intestate Estate.

THE RIGHTS OF A CHILD

THE NON-MARITAL CHILD

A child born out of wedlock has the same rights to inherit from his/her biological father as one born in wedlock, provided any one of the following are true:

☑   Both parents sign a notarized statement that acknowledges his paternity.

☑   He and the child's mother were married within 10 months (before or after) the child's birth.

☑   Genetic testing shows that he is the father to degree of at least 95% probability.

☑   The child's birth certificate is signed by the father and mother (ARS 25-814).

If the decedent denied he is the child's father, it will take a court procedure to establish (or disprove) paternity If the parent did not treat a child as his own, and refused to support the child, the parent will lose his right to inherit the child's property (ARS 14-2114C).

THE ADOPTED CHILD

An adopted child has the same right to inherit property under Arizona's Laws of Intestate Succession from his adoptive parents as does their biological child. The adopted child has no right to inherit from his biological parents, with the exception of the parent who is married to the adoptive parent. For example, is adopted by a step-parent, the child has the right to inherit from his natural parents and from his adoptive parent as well (ARS 8-117).

THE AFTERBORN CHILD

Under Arizona law a child conceived prior to death and born to the surviving spouse after the death has the same right to inherit as any other natural child of the decedent, provided the child lives at least 120 hours (5 days) after its birth (ARS 14-2108).

WHO DIED FIRST?

Sometimes it happens that two family members die simultaneously, and no one knows who died first. For example, suppose a husband and wife die together in a car crash, how is their property distributed in that case?

Arizona law provides for an orderly distribution of those who die simultaneously:

PROCEEDS OF A LIFE INSURANCE POLICY
Suppose the husband is insured, with his wife as the beneficiary of his life insurance policy. If they die simultaneously, the proceeds of the policy will be distributed as if the wife died before her husband. The proceeds will be given to the alternate beneficiary named in the policy, unless some other provision was made (ARS 20-1127).

THE 120 HOUR RULE
As explained earlier, the beneficiary of property located in Arizona must live at least 120 hours more than the decedent in order to inherit his property. If the decedent and his beneficiary die simultaneously, the property is distributed as if the beneficiary died first (ARS 14-2104).

JOINTLY OWNED PROPERTY
The 120 hour rule applies to property owned Jointly With Right of Survivorship. If no provision is made for the simultaneous death of the co-owners, the property is divided with half going to the Estate of each owner (ARS 14-2702).

Under Arizona law anyone who is found guilty of the murder of the decedent is prohibited from profiting from the crime. Property that the killer, would have inherited as a beneficiary of the decedent's Will or according to the Arizona Laws of Intestate Succession, will be distributed as if the killer died before the decedent.

Upon the Court determination of guilt, property that was owned by the decedent and the killer, as Jointly With Right of Survivorship, becomes a Tenancy In Common, insofar as the killer and the decedent are concerned. Any other person who is a joint owner of the property, remains a joint owner. Similarly if the killer is a beneficiary of the decedents life insurance policy or annuity, whoever is named as alternate beneficiary will inherit the insurance proceeds (ARS 14-2803).

 **☎ LAWYER** | LAW SUIT FOR WRONGFUL DEATH

If anyone caused an injury to the decedent that was related to his death, then regardless of whether that person is convicted of a crime, the Personal Representative may sue that person for a wrongful death on behalf of the beneficiaries of the decedent's Estate. See Chapter 1 for a discussion of a wrongful death.

WHEN TO CHALLENGE THE WILL

It is not uncommon for a family member to be unhappy with the way the decedent willed his property. If you are tempted to challenge a Will, first consider whether the Will is valid under Arizona law. In Arizona, a Will is presumed valid if at the time the decedent made the Will he was at least 18 years of age and of sound mind (ARS 14-2501). Arizona Courts have ruled that a person is of "sound mind" if at the time he made the Will he knew:

⇨ what he was doing (namely making a Will), and

⇨ what property he owned, and

⇨ who of his relatives would, under ordinary circumstances, expect to inherit that property

(*Evans v Liston*, 116 Ariz. 218 (App. 1977); 568 P.2d 1116).

⊠ **THE UNWITNESSED WILL**

The first step in the Probate procedure is to have the Probate court determine whether the Will presented is valid. If the Will is in writing and signed by the Will maker in the presence of at least two credible witnesses, there should be no problem in having the Will accepted into Probate. But suppose the decedent wrote out a Will in his own hand and signed it when no one was present? A Will written in the Will maker's hand is called a **holographic Will**. The state of Arizona recognizes such a Will as being valid, providing the signature and the main parts of the Will are in the handwriting of the decedent (ARS 14-2503).

But the problem with a holographic Will is its authenticity. Because no one saw the decedent sign the Will, it is hard to determine whether the Will was written by the decedent or is a forgery. If all the decedent left was a holographic Will, you might consider consulting with an attorney experienced in Probate matters.

⊠   THE WILL WITNESSED BY A BENEFICIARY

Having the Will witnessed usually solves the problem of authenticity; but if either witness is a beneficiary of the Will, someone may accuse the witness of pressuring the Will maker into giving the gift. But, under Arizona law just the fact that the witness to the Will is also a beneficiary of your Will does not automatically make the Will or the gift invalid (ARS 14-2505).

⊠   UNDUE INFLUENCE

Those who receive a lesser gift, might accuse the witness/ beneficiary of using *undue influence* to get the Will maker give him the gift. Undue influence occurs whenever some- one exerts such pressure on the Will maker so that he is not acting according to his own free will.

But undue influence is not easily proved. Arizona courts take many things into consideration when determining whether there was undue influence. The Court is likely to find undue influence if it can be proven that:

⇨   there was a confidential relationship between
the Will maker and the beneficiary (close relative,
spiritual advisor, attorney, financial advisor,
doctor, etc.) AND

⇨   the beneficiary was active in getting the Will
maker to sign the Will AND

⇨   the person using such influence is a principal
beneficiary of the Will
(*Evans v Liston*, 116 Ariz. 218 (App. 1977); 568 P.2d 1116).

☒ THE VERBAL WILL

Picture a death bed scene. The elderly gentleman is surrounded by several family members. In a whisper, just audible enough to be heard, he says: "Even though I am a wealthy man, I never got around to making a Will. You all have been good to me, but I did want my entire fortune to go to my nephew, Robert. He has been like a son to me. "

Do you think Robert can inherit his Uncle's Estate?
Not in Arizona unless:
⇨ The uncle writes out his Will in his own hand

- or -

⇨ Someone writes down his wishes and he signs the document acknowledging it as his last Will

- or -

⇨ Someone signs the Will on behalf of the Uncle and by his direction, and at least two people sign the Will as witnesses (ARS 14-2502).

Considering that the uncle's relatives will probably inherit the fortune under the Arizona's Laws of Intestate Succession, it is doubtful that Robert is in danger of becoming wealthy at any time in the near future.

☒ THE WILL THAT IS CONTRARY TO LAW

Sometimes a person who is of sound mind, makes a Will, but that Will has the effect of giving a spouse or a minor child less than is required under Arizona law. One such example is that of Nancy. Hers was not an easy life. She worked long hours as a waitress. She divorced her hard drinking first husband. The final judgment gave her their homestead, some securities, and sole custody of their son. After the divorce Nancy had her attorney prepare a Will leaving all she owned to her son, Richard.

Some years later she met and married Harry, a chef at the restaurant where she worked. He moved into her home and they later had twin daughters. Richard was 19, and his half-sisters 12, when Nancy died after a lengthy battle with cancer.

Nancy did not leave much — her home, the securities, now worth $50,000, which were in Nancy's name only.

Before she died, she told Richard, that she had not changed her Will because she wanted him to have all she owned. She said Harry had a good job and she was sure he would take good care of his daughters.

No sooner was the funeral over, when Richard came in and demanded that Harry vacate his mother's home.

Nancy never discussed her Will with Harry, so he was surprised, and angry, when he learned that she wanted everything she had to go to Richard. He was so upset, he went to an attorney.

"I took good care of Nancy all these years, and yet she didn't even consider leaving something to me or to our daughters. She always favored Richard over the girls. It just isn't right."

The lawyer explained Arizona law:
"Your wife wrote her Will before she married you. Under Arizona statute 14-2301, you have no right to challenge the Will because she gave her property to her son. But your daughters are entitled to share equally in property given to Richard. Under Arizona statute 14-2302, any child who is born after the decedent executed the Will is entitled to a share of the Estate unless the decedent gave all of her property to the parent of the omitted child. In this case Sylvia gave all of her property to Richard and not to you, so the girls are entitled to an equal share of Sylvia's estate.

Although you have no grounds to challenge Nancy's Will on your own behalf, you are still entitled to a Homestead Allowance of $18,000 and up to $7,000 in value of her household furniture; appliances and personal effects. But, a person can waive (give up) his rights in the Homestead Allowance and Exempt property (ARS 14-2207). Did you sign any Premarital or Postmarital Agreement giving up these rights?"

"Absolutely not. What about the twins? Are they entitled to a Homestead Allowance?"

The attorney explained "They are not entitled to a Homestead Allowance; however, they are entitled to a Family Allowance for their maintenance during Probate because Sylvia contributed to their support up till the time she became too ill to work. I see no point in asking for it because Arizona statute 14-2404 makes any amount the girls receive as a Family Allowance to be set off against the amount they receive as a beneficiary of the Will."

Richard did not fare as well as his mother intended. The securities had to be sold to pay for Nancy's funeral expenses, medical bills, and the costs of probating the Estate, including the Homestead Allowance. All that Richard inherited was his one-third share of the house. And he didn't get the proceeds of the sale of the house until it was all sold at the end of the year.

No doubt Nancy did not understand what would happen to her Estate once she passed on. Had Sylvia known about Arizona law, she could have transferred her securities, cash and car to her son before she died. She was free to do so when she was alive because these items belonged to her as Separate Property.

But the moral of the story, for the purpose of this discussion, is that if you believe that the decedent's Will is not valid or drafted according to Arizona law, then you need to consult with an attorney experienced in Probate matters to determine your legal rights under that Will.

Getting Possession Of The Property 6

Knowing who is entitled to receive the decedent's property is one thing. Getting that property is another. As explained in the previous chapter, if the decedent held property Jointly With Right of Survivorship, or in trust for someone, the property now belongs to the joint owner or beneficiary. If it is personal property such as a bank account or a security, the beneficiary can usually get possession of the property by giving a certified copy of the death certificate to the financial institution, with the understanding that if money is needed to pay the decedent's debts, the joint owner or beneficiary will return the decedent's share to his Estate (ARS 14-6215).

.

If the decedent had real or personal property in his name only, or if he held property as a Tenant In Common, some sort of Probate proceeding may be necessary in order to transfer ownership to the proper beneficiary. The assistance of an attorney may be required should a full Probate proceeding be necessary, but there are many items that can be transferred without legal assistance. This chapter explains how to get possession of those items.

The chapter also contains an explanation of the different kinds of Probate procedures and when it is appropriate to use that procedure.

DISTRIBUTING PERSONAL PROPERTY

Too often, the first person to discover the body will help himself to the decedent's *personal effects* (clothing, jewelry, appliances, electrical equipment, cameras, books, stamp or coin collection, household items and furnishing, etc.). Unless that person is the decedent's sole beneficiary, such action is unconscionable, if not illegal. The decedent's personal effects should be given to the person appointed as the Personal Representative to be distributed according to the decedent's Will, or if no Will according to the Arizona Laws of Intestate Succession.

As explained in Chapter 4, the decedent's spouse, or if no spouse, his children are entitled to keep up to $7,000 in household furnishings and appliances free from the claims of creditors (ARS 14-2403).

The decedent may have left a writing making gifts of his *tangible personal property* (clothing, jewelry, etc.). To be distributed as part of a Probate proceeding, the writing needs to be referred to in the Will. The writing needs to be in the decedent's own hand or if the gift was made by means of a typewritten statement, his signature needs to appear at the end of the document. In addition, the statement or list needs to describe the item and the beneficiary of the gift, with reasonable certainty (ARS 14-2513).

If Probate is not necessary, his next of kin, as determined by the Laws of Intestate Succession, need to divide all of the personal effects among themselves in approximately equal proportions.

What's Equal?

The decedent's Will may direct that the decedent's personal property be divided equally between two or more beneficiaries. The problem with the term "equal" is that people have different ideas of what "equal" means. Unless there is clear evidence that the decedent's Will meant something else, "equal" refers to the monetary value of the item and not to the number of items received. For example, to divide the decedent's personal effects equally, one beneficiary may receive an expensive item of jewelry and another beneficiary may receive several items whose overall value is approximately equal to that single piece of jewelry.

When distributing personal effects there needs to be cooperation and perhaps compromise, or else bitter arguments might arise over items of little monetary value. One such argument occurred when an elderly woman died who was rich only in her love for her five children and ten grandchildren. After the funeral, the children gathered in their mother's apartment. Each child had his/her own furnishings and no need for anything in the apartment. They agreed to donate all of their mother's personal effects to a local charity with the exception of a few items of sentimental value.

Each child took some small item as a remembrance — a handkerchief, a large platter that their mother used to serve family dinners, a doily their mother crocheted. Things went smoothly until it came to her photograph album. Frank, the youngest sibling, said, "I'll take this." Marie objected saying "But there are pictures in the album that I want."

Frank retorted, "You already took all the pictures Mom had on her dresser."

The argument went downhill from there. Unsettled sibling rivalries boiled over, fueled by the hurt of the loss that they were all experiencing. It almost came to blows when the eldest settled the argument: "Frank you make copies of all of the photos in the album for Marie. Marie, you make copies of all of the pictures that you took and give them to Frank. This way you both will have a complete set of Mom's pictures. And while you're at it, make copies for the rest of us."

NONPROBATE TRANSFERS

A **nonprobate transfer** is a transfer of the decedent's property without the need for Probate. For example, if the decedent had a bank account in his name only "in trust for" someone or with instructions to "pay on death" to someone, all the beneficiary need do is produce a death certificate and proper identification, and the bank will turn over the property to the beneficiary. Securities that are held jointly with someone, or with instructions to "transfer on death" to a named beneficiary, can be transferred to that beneficiary in the same manner (ARS 14-6212, 14-6222).

There are other items that can be transferred to the proper beneficiary without the need for Probate. For a married decedent, his final paycheck is one of them.

THE DECEDENT'S FINAL PAYCHECK
The decedent's spouse can use an Affidavit to collect the decedent's last pay check, provided the check is not greater than $5,000 (ARS 14-3971(A)). An **Affidavit** is a written statement of facts. The **Affiant** (the person making the statement) must sign the Affidavit in the presence of a notary public and take an oath or affirm that the facts, as written, are true.

The spouse does not need to wait any period of time and can submit the Affidavit to the employer whenever it is convenient. The following is a sample Affidavit

---

AFFIDAVIT PURSUANT TO
ARIZONA STATUTE 14-3971(A)

I, _____ (name of spouse) being first duly sworn, on oath, deposes and says:

1. The decedent _____(name) died on_____ (date) at the county of _____ state of _____.

2.   Affiant is the surviving spouse of the decedent and is entitled to receive from the decedent's employer, any wage, salary or other compensation due to the decedent, not in excess of $5,000.

3.   An application or petition for the appointment of a personal representative is not pending or has not been granted in any jurisdiction, or if granted, the personal representative has been discharged or more than one year has elapsed since a closing statement has been filed.

This affidavit is made pursuant to Section 14-3971 (A), Arizona Revised Statutes, as amended, for the purpose of making claim decedent's wages, salary or compensation under said statute.

Affiant Name _____

Affiant Signature _____ date_____

Subscribed and sworn to before me this date _____ at _____ County, state of _____

_____
Notary Signature and Seal

If the value of the decedent's personal property is $50,000, or less, (not counting the final paycheck paid to his spouse) the beneficiary can get possession of the decedent's securities (stock, bond, CD, bank account) by giving the bank or financial institution an Affidavit.

The statute requires the beneficiary to verify that all the following are true:

30 DAYS PASSED
At least 30 days have passed since the decedent's death.

NO PENDING PROBATE PROCEDURE
No one has petitioned to become Personal Representative or if a Personal Representative has been appointed, at least one year has passed since he filed a closing statement with the court.

AFFIANT IS THE SUCCESSOR TO THE PROPERTY
The Affiant must be entitled to the property either because the decedent left the property to him by Will or because he inherits the property under Arizona's Laws of Intestate Succession.

DECEDENT'S PERSONAL PROPERTY IS $50,000 OR LESS
The decedent's personal property is everything he owns in this state or elsewhere, not including any real property that he may own. The value of his personal property as of his date of death, less any money he might own on his personal property, cannot exceed $50,000 (ARS 14-3971).

The Affidavit is a good vehicle to use if all that needs to be done is to transfer a few items and the decedent's Estate does not exceed $50,000. But sometimes it happens that the decedent has a small estate and there is much that needs to be done. In such case it may be better to have a Personal Representative appointed who can do all of the following:

FILE TAX RETURNS
A final tax return needs to be filed and perhaps a tax refund given to the proper beneficiary.

PAY BILLS
Bills may need to be paid to many different creditors (telephone bills, credit cards, medical bills, rent payments, car lease payments, etc.)

DISTRIBUTE PROPERTY
Property may need to be distributed to several different beneficiaries after all the bills are paid.

GIVE NOTICE TO CREDITORS
An important reason to appoint a Personal Representative is to start the Statute of Limitations clock ticking. If the Personal Representative notifies a creditor, in writing, of the death, and the creditor does not present his claim within 60 days after the mailing, or 4 months after the Personal Representative publishes notice (whichever is later), the creditor's claim is forever barred (ARS 14-3801).

Without notice from the Personal Representative, creditors have two years from the date of death to demand payment from whoever has possession of the decedent's property (ARS 14-3803).

As explained in chapter 5, if the decedent held the car jointly with another and title to the car reads "AND/OR" or "OR," The joint owner now owns the car. The surviving owner needs to contact the Motor Vehicle Division and remove the decedent's name from the title.

If the decedent owned the car with another and the title reads "AND," the decedent's half goes to whomever he named in his Will. If he died intestate, his half goes to his next of kin as determined in the Arizona Law of Intestate Succession. If Probate is necessary, it becomes the job of the Personal Representative to transfer the car to the proper beneficiary. The surviving spouse has the right to keep up to $7,000 of the Exempt Property listed on page 106. That list includes an automobile titled in the decedent's name. If the surviving spouse does not want the car, or if the decedent was single, the Personal Representative will transfer the car according to the terms of the Will. If the Will makes a *specific gift* of the car, the Personal Representative will transfer the car to that person. If there was no mention of the car in the decedent's Will, it goes to the *residuary beneficiaries* under the Will, i.e., those who inherit the *Residuary Estate* (i.e., whatever is left once all debts, taxes, costs of administration are paid and special gifts distributed). If the decedent ent did not have a Will, the car goes to the decedent's heirs as determined by the Laws of Intestate Succession.

TRANSFER WHEN MORE THAN ONE BENEFICIARY

If there is more than one person who has the right to inherit the car, they all can take title to the car. That may not be a practical thing to do since only one person can drive the car at any given time and if one gets into an accident, they all can be held liable.

The better route is for the beneficiaries to agree to have one person take title to the car. The person taking title will need to compensate the others for their share of the car. In such case the beneficiaries need to come to an agreement as to the value of the car.

DETERMINING THE VALUE OF THE CAR

Cars are valued in different ways. The *collateral* value of the car is the value that banks use to evaluate the car for purposes of making a loan to the owner of the car. If you were to trade in a car for the purpose of purchasing a new one, the car dealer would offer you its *wholesale* value. Were you to purchase that same car from a car dealer, he would price it at its *retail* or *fair market value*. Usually the retail price is highest, wholesale is lowest and its collateral value is somewhere in between.

You can call your local bank to get the collateral value of the car. It may be more difficult to obtain the wholesale value because the amount of money a dealer is willing to pay depends on the value of the new car that you are purchasing. You can determine the car's retail value by looking at comparable used car advertisements in the local newspaper.

Rather than going through the effort of determining these three values, you can use your Internet search engine to look up the Kelley Blue Book Value. The Website gives Low, Average and High Blue Book Values which correspond to the wholesale, collateral and retail values.

Once the fair market value of the car is determined, the beneficiary who takes the car will be considered to have received that value as part of his inheritance. If none of the beneficiaries want the car, the Personal Representative will sell it and add the proceeds to the amount distributed to the beneficiaries.

It is a good idea to limit the use of the car until it is sold or transferred to the beneficiary. If the decedent's car is involved in an accident before the car is transferred to the new owner, the decedent's Estate may be liable for the damage. Having adequate insurance on the car may save the Estate from monetary loss, but a pending lawsuit could delay Probate and prevent any money from being distributed to the beneficiaries until the lawsuit is settled.

🚗 MAKING THE TRANSFER 🚐

You will need the original motor vehicle title in order to transfer a motor vehicle. See page 67 if you cannot locate the title. Arizona statute 14-3971 (D) provides for the transfer of a motor vehicle on presentation of an Affidavit. The Motor Vehicle Division will give you the Affidavit (Motor Vehicle Division form 32-6901 RO7/98) at the same time they give you the Title and Registration application form. To make the transfer by Affidavit, the same rules apply as with the transfer of securities (page 147) namely:

⇨ At least 30 days have passed since death of decedent

⇨ Decedent's personal property does not exceed $50,000

⇨ No appointment of Personal Representative, or at least one year has passed since closing statement filed

⇨ Affiant is the proper successor to the motor vehicle.

You can get information about making the transfer and the location of your nearest Customer Service Center from the Motor Vehicle Division section of the Arizona Department of Transportation Website.

 ARIZONA DEPARTMENT OF TRANSPORTATION
http://www.azdot.gov/mvd

Arizona requires that the owner of a motor vehicle be insured for bodily injury and property damage (ARS 28-4009). Before making the transfer, have the new owner show proof of insurance. After making the transfer, verify that the new owner is the registered owner according to the records of the Motor Vehicle Division. Once the registration is changed, contact the decedent's insurance company and arrange to have the decedent's motor vehicle policy cancelled. The company should refund any unused premium to the decedent's Estate.

NOTIFY THE MOTOR VEHICLE DIVISION OF THE TRANSFER

Once you have transferred the motor vehicle, or if you have terminated the decedent's car lease, it is important to notify the Motor Vehicle Division of the transfer so that the decedent's Estate will no longer be liable for tickets or accidents. The Personal Representative or next of kin can do so by writing to:

Mail Drop 555M
Motor Vehicle Division
P.O. Box 2100
Phoenix AZ 85001

and notifying them of the name of the new owner, his/her name and address, the Decedent's name, and the date the vehicle was transferred.

The leased car is not an asset of the Estate because the decedent did not own the car. The decedent was obligated to pay the balance of the monies owed on the lease agreement, so the car is a liability to the Estate. The Personal Representative needs to work out an agreement with the company to either assign the lease tosomeone who agrees to pay the balance of the lease — or have the Estate pay off the lease by purchasing the car under the terms of the lease agreement.

Some lenders will allow the lease to be assigned provided the Estate remains liable for the balance of payment. In such cases, it is better to have the car refinanced and have the original lease paid in full.

If the remaining payments exceed the current market value of the car, there may be a temptation to hand the keys over to the leasing company. This may not be the best strategy, because the leasing company can sell the car and then sue the Estate for the balance of the monies owed. If the decedent had no assets or if the only assets he had are creditor proof, simply returning the car may be an option. But if the decedent's Estate has assets available to pay the balance of the lease payments, the Personal Representative needs to arrange to have the car transferred in a way that releases the Estate from all further liability.

TRANSFERRING THE MOBILE/MANUFACTURED HOME

A motorized home is a motor vehicle, so it is transferred in the same manner as any other motor vehicle. A mobile home that is permanently attached to the land is another story. As explained in Chapter 3, a mobile/manufactured home is registered with the County Assessor and is treated much same as any other residential property. If you inherited the mobile/manufactured home, you need to notify the County Assessor of the change of ownership.

You need to determine whether the land on which the mobile home is located was leased or owned by the decedent. If the decedent was renting space in a trailer park, you need to contact the trailer park owner to transfer the lease to your name.

If the decedent owned the land under the mobile/manufactured home, the land and the home need to be transferred. Hopefully, the decedent gave the land and the home to the same beneficiary. If not, the beneficiary of the mobile/manufactured home will need to come to some sort of agreement with the owner of the land. If the land owner does not wish to allow the mobile/manufactured home to remain on his land, the beneficiary will need to make arrangements to have the home moved to another location.

If the same person inherited the land and the home, he will need to have title to the land transferred to his name. A discussion of how to transfer the land to the proper beneficiary is discussed later in this Chapter.

TRANSFERRING AIRCRAFT

As explained in Chapter 3, the Civil Aviation Registry of the Federal Aviation Administration ("FAA") is in charge of the ownership and security documents filed with the FAA. The Personal Representative will need to contact them at (405) 954-3116 for information about transferring title to the proper beneficiary. The new owner of the aircraft will need to register the plane with the FAA. If the airplane is to be based or primarily used within Arizona, he will also need to register the aircraft with the Aeronautics Division of the Arizona Department of Transportation within 60 days of the date of transfer (ARS 28-8332).

If you are the new owner of the aircraft you can call the Aeronautics Division at (602) 294-9144 to obtain forms to register the plane, or you can write to them at:

ADOT AERONAUTICS DIVISION
255 East Osborn Road, Suite 101
Phoenix, AZ   85012

Forms and Information are also available at their Website.

 ARIZONA DEPARTMENT OF TRANSPORTATION
AERONAUTICS DIVISION
http://www.azdot.gov/aviation

TRANSFERRING WATERCRAFT

Motorboats operated within the state of Arizona must be registered with Arizona Game & Fish. To transfer the watercraft to the proper beneficiary, the Personal Representative needs to issue a bill of sale to the beneficiary. The new owner must obtain his own Annual Decal and Certificate of Number (ARS 5-321). He can do so by taking the bill of sale to the nearest Arizona Game & Fish office.

If you are the beneficiary of the boat, you can call (602) 942-3000 for information about making the transfer and the location of the office nearest you.

You can also get this information by visiting the Arizona Game & Fish Website.

 ARIZONA GAME & FISH
http://www.gf.state.az.us

THE FEDERAL INCOME TAX REFUND

Any refund due to the decedent under a joint federal income tax return filed by his surviving spouse will be sent to the surviving spouse. If the decedent's Personal Representative filed the final return, the refund check will be sent to him to be deposited to the Estate account.

If the decedent was single and no Probate proceeding is necessary, whoever is entitled to the decedent's Estate is entitled to the refund check. If you are the beneficiary of the decedent's Estate, you can obtain the refund by filing IRS form 1310 along with the decedent's final income tax return (the 1040).

You can obtain form 1310 from the decedent's accountant, or if he did not have an accountant and you wish to file yourself, you can call the IRS at (800) 829-3676 to obtain the form.

You can download instructions, publications and forms from the Internal Revenue Service by going to the **FORMS AND PUBLICATIONS** section of their Website.

 INTERNAL REVENUE SERVICE
http://www.irs.gov/

The Personal Representative does not need to file form 1310 because once he files the decedent's final income tax return, any refund will be forwarded to him. Similarly, it is not necessary for the surviving spouse who filed a joint return to file form 1310.

THE ARIZONA INCOME TAX REFUND

The decedent's final Arizona income tax return needs to be filed with the Arizona Department of Revenue at the same time the federal income tax return is filed (ARS 43-325). If the decedent was married, his spouse can file a joint return. If he was single, the Personal Representative will file the return. If Probate is not necessary, whoever takes possession of the decedent's property can file the final income tax return.

If a refund is due, you will need to complete Arizona form 131: Claim For Refund on Behalf of Deceased Taxpayer

If you have any question about filing the decedent's final return, call the Arizona Department of Revenue toll free at (877) 492-9957. You can download forms and get information about filing a return at the Arizona Department of Revenue Website. http://www.azdor.gov

DEPOSITING THE TAX REFUND

If the decedent was not married, and the Personal Representative filed the final return, the refund check will be sent to him to be deposited into the Estate account. If Probate is not necessary and the refund check (or any other check) is in the name of the decedent, you can deposit it into the decedent's bank account. You can get the money in the decedent's account by using whatever Probate procedure is appropriate.

No Probate procedure is necessary to transfer real property if the decedent held that property as:

⇨   the owner of a Life Estate - or -

⇨   the Grantor of a Beneficiary Deed - or -

⇨   a Joint Tenant With Right of Survivorship - or -

⇨   Community Property With Right of Survivorship.

In each of these cases, the surviving Grantee owns the property as of the date of death, however, the decedent's name remains on the deed. Anyone examining title to the property will not know of the death. Arizona Office of Vital Records is responsible to issue the death certificate, but not to publish it or make it part of the public record.

Of course, if there is a Probate proceeding, anyone can look up those public records and learn of the death. If no Probate is necessary and you are the beneficiary of a Beneficiary Deed, or the owner of the remainder interest in a Life Estate, you need to have a certified copy of the death certificate recorded in the county where the property is located to let everyone know that you now own the property.

If you are the surviving joint owner and have a right of survivorship, your attorney can draft an **AFFIDAVIT OF TERMINATION OF JOINT TENANCY INTEREST** for you to sign. Once the Affidavit, and the death certificate along with it, are recorded, the decedent's name is, in effect, removed from the deed.

Recording the death certificate or an Affidavit "removes" the decedent's name from the deed, but there is still the problem of proving that he didn't owe any taxes.

Should you later sell the property, the buyer will want to be assured that there are no Arizona Taxes that might become a lien on the property as a result of the decedent's death. The closing could be delayed while the closing agent scrambles to obtain a tax release from the Arizona Department of Revenue.

To avoid the problem, you can have your attorney apply for a **WAIVER OF ESTATE TAXES** from the Department of Revenue. When the Waiver is received the attorney can have it recorded along with the death certificate and Affidavit. Once these documents are recorded, you can sell or transfer the property at any time without delay.

Even if you don't intend to sell or transfer the property during your lifetime, it is important that you take care of these matters soon after the decedent's death, otherwise you might be leaving a problem for your beneficiaries. Whoever inherits your property will need to obtain tax clearance for you and for the decedent. That might be difficult to do if many years have passed since the decedent's death.

If the decedent owned property as a Tenant In Common or in his name only, some document will need to be recorded that identities the beneficiary and new owner of the property. If Probate is necessary, the Personal Representative will transfer the decedent's real property to the proper beneficiary. If the decedent's Estate is worth 50,000 or less, the beneficiary can get possession of the real property by signing an *Affidavit Of Succession of Real Property* prepared according to Arizona statute (ARS 14-3971(E)).

The Affidavit verifies that all of the following are true:

PROPERTY NOT MORE THAN $50,000
The value of all of the decedent's interest in real property owned in the state of Arizona is not greater than $50,000. The value of the property is computed by taking the amount shown on the assessment rolls for the year in which the decedent died, less any monies owed on that property. For example, suppose the decedent and his brother owned a condominium as Tenants In Common, with each owning half of the property. If the assessed value of the property is $120,000 and there is a mortgage of $50,000, the brothers have $70,000 equity in the property. The decedent's share is worth $35,000. In such case, whoever inherits the decedent's share can get title to the property by filing the Affidavit with the Court.

AT LEAST 6 MONTHS HAVE PASSED SINCE DATE OF DEATH
A transfer of real property by means of Affidavit cannot be made sooner than six months from the date of the decedent's death.

NO PENDING PROBATE PROCEDURE

No one has petitioned to become Personal Representative or if a Personal Representative has been appointed, at least one year has passed since he filed a closing statement with the Probate Court.

NO ESTATE TAXES DUE

There is no federal or Arizona Estate Tax due on the decedent's estate.

ALL UNSECURED DEBTS PAID

The funeral expenses, and expenses of the decedent's last illness have been paid. All the decedent's *unsecured* debts have been paid. If the decedent has a mortgage on his home, then that is a *secured* debt. A chattel mortgage on a car is also a secured debt. The creditor of a secured debt is assured of the payment of the debt or the creditor can take possession of the property. An unsecured creditor has no safety net, so Arizona law does not allow the decedent's property to be given to a beneficiary until all unsecured creditors are paid.

AFFIANT IS ENTITLED TO THE PROPERTY

The person who signs the Affidavit must be entitled to the property for any one of the following reasons:

➢ Affiant is the heir of the property according to the Arizona Law of Intestate Succession.

➢ Affiant is taking the property instead of taking Exempt Property or a Homestead or Family allowance

➢ The decedent named the Affiant as the beneficiary of the property in his last Will

NO ONE ELSE IS ENTITLED TO THE PROPERTY

The decedent was the rightful owner of the property and no one other than Affiant has a right to the property (ARS 14-3971(E)).

If all of these statements are true, the property can be transferred by means of an Affidavit. For the transfer to be effective, it will need to be recorded in the county in which the property is located, but the County Recorder will not record the Affidavit unless the Probate Court approves the transfer and issues a certified copy of the Affidavit. Bottom line — you still need to get permission from the Probate Court.

If you know your way around the courthouse or if you are an enthusiastic "do it yourselfer," you may want to try to navigate the Probate procedure on your own. Your first stop will be the Superior Court in the county where the decedent had his residence. If the decedent was not a resident of Arizona, you need go to the Superior Court in the county where the property is located.

There is a section within the courthouse called the Quick Court. You can pick up the proper Affidavit form from the Probate Registrar, who is a non-judicial, court official. You will need to pay a filing fee, so you may wish to first call and ask how much you will pay and what documents you need to bring with you. Once the Affidavit is approved by the Probate Registrar, the clerk of the Probate Court will issue a certified copy of the Affidavit. You will need to take the certified copy to the office of the Recorder in the county in which the property is located.

As you can see this is a somewhat involved procedure. If you make a mistake such as copying the legal description of the property incorrectly on the Affidavit, you might need to employ an attorney to fix the problem. A mistake can cost you more money than if you had employed an attorney in the first place. You might save yourself time and maybe even money, if you consult with an attorney before trying to transfer ownership of real property by means of Affidavit.

Each state regulates the transfer of real property within that state. Many states, like Arizona, do not require that any document be recorded to transfer real property to a joint tenant who has a right of survivorship, or to the owner of the remainder interest of a Life Estate. All the Grantee need do is keep a certified copy of the death certificate available to produce at closing when the property is transferred.

Some states allow the death certificate to be recorded in the county where the property is located, so that anyone examining title to the property will know who now owns the property. In other states, an Affidavit is recorded along with the death certificate that identifies the current owner of the property.

If the decedent owned out of state real property Jointly With Right of Survivorship, or if he held a Life Estate interest, you may want to call the recording department in the county where the property is located to find out what documents (if any) need to be recorded to let people know that the Grantee now owns the property. In Arizona, the County Recorder is in charge of recording deeds. In other states, it might be the Clerk of the Circuit Court, or the County Registrar.

Of course, if the decedent owned real property in his own name only or as a Tenant In Common, you need to contact an attorney in that state to have the property transferred to the proper beneficiary.

A SIMPLIFIED PROBATE PROCEDURE

Arizona statute (ARS 14-3973) allows a simplified Probate procedure called SUMMARY ADMINISTRATION for small Estates. The statute does not give a dollar amount for the procedure, but requires that the total value of the decedent's Estate not exceed the sum of the following:

- ⇨ reasonable funeral expenses
- ⇨ Homestead Allowance ($18,000)
- ⇨ Family Allowance ($12,000)
- ⇨ Exempt Property ($7,000)
- ⇨ Costs and expenses of administration
- ⇨ reasonable and necessary medical and hospital expenses of the decedent's last illness.

The cost of a person's last illness, alone, could be in the hundreds of thousands of dollars, but the Summary Administrative procedure was not designed to handle large Estates. As a rule of thumb, if the entire value of the decedent's Estate (less monies owed on any of the property) is greater than $50,000, consult with an attorney experienced in Probate matter to determine whether a formal Probate Administration is the better route to go.

The first step in the Summary Administration procedure is to have someone appointed by the court as Personal Representative. The person named as Personal Representative or Executor of the Will has priority. If there is no Will the surviving spouse, or if no spouse, whoever is entitled to inherit the property can be appointed as Personal Representative. The Summary Administration procedure is designed to settle an Estate that has no problems associated with it, so if there is any disagreement about who is to serve as Personal Representative, this is not the way to go.

Similarly, Summary Administration was not designed to deal with disputes about whether a claim against the Estate should be paid. A *Formal Probate* procedure is necessary if there is any dispute associated with the settlement of the Estate with a hearing on the matter and notice to all interested parties (ARS 14-1401, 14-1403).

Whoever is going to be appointed Personal Representative for the Summary Administration, needs to apply to the Probate Court in the county of the decedent's residence. If the decedent was not a resident of the state, the Probate proceeding may be conducted the county where the decedent owned property (ARS 14-3201).

If you are going to apply for Summary Administration, you may save time by first calling the Registrar and asking:
How do I get to the courthouse?
When is the best time to meet with the Registrar?
What documents should I bring?
How much money should I bring for the filing fee?

Once the Registrar is satisfied that the Estate qualifies for Summary Administration he will issue Letters of Administration. With these Letters you can go about the business of paying bills, and then distributing whatever is left to the beneficiaries of the Estate. Once you complete these tasks, you need to file a closing statement with the Court verifying that you have fully administered the Estate. You will need to send a copy of the closing statement to each beneficiary of the Estate and to any unpaid creditor of the Estate.

If there are no law suits involving you as Personal Representative within a year following the filing of the closing statement, the Court will discharge you and the Probate will be closed (ARS 14-3974).

YOUR RIGHTS AS A BENEFICIARY

There will need to be a Probate proceeding if the decedent left personal property in excess of $50,000 or real property in excess of $50,000. The proceeding can take anywhere from several months to more than a year depending on the size and complexity of the Probate Estate. A Personal Representative must be appointed and Letters issued.

The Personal Representative is in charge of settling the Estate. Too often, beneficiaries of the Estate have no idea what is going on. They wait to receive their inheritance, not knowing that they have rights under Arizona law; and more importantly, not knowing how to assert their rights.

✧ RIGHT TO BE KEPT INFORMED

Anyone who has an interest in the Estate has the right to be kept informed, provided that person asserts his right by filing a **DEMAND FOR NOTICE** with the Probate Court in the county of the decedent's residence. The Notice will give your name, address and the nature of your interest in the Estate. Filing a Demand For Notice ensures that you will be notified as soon as someone begins the Probate procedure, and you will receive a copy of any order or document that is filed in this case.

You can file your Demand For Notice any time after the decedent's death. It is important to do so as soon as possible, so that you can raise any objection you may have in a timely manner (ARS 14-3204).

✧ RIGHT TO OBJECT TO PERSONAL REPRESENTATIVE

As discussed earlier, if the decedent died without a Will, the surviving spouse has the right to be Personal Representative. If the spouse is unable or unwilling to serve, or if the decedent was single, whoever is entitled to inherit his property under the Arizona Laws of Intestate Succession can ask to be appointed as Personal Representative (ARS 14-3203).

The Court has final say as to who will serve as Personal Representative. The judge can appoint the person with priority, or if the majority of the beneficiaries of the Estate request another person, he can appoint that person. If you object to the person who is asking to be appointed, you can raise these concerns with the Court, however, it may take a Formal Probate procedure to settle the matter. Formal Probate proceedings can be costly to the Estate as well as to the person who is raising the objection. Before expressing your objection to the Court, it is important to consult with an experienced Probate attorney.

He can explain the best way for you to present your concerns to the Court. He can tell you what arguments have a good chance of swaying the judge. And he can tell you which arguments have so little probability of success that they are not worth pursuing.

✧ RIGHT TO YOUR OWN ATTORNEY

The attorney who handles the Estate is employed by, and represents, the Personal Representative. If the Estate is sizeable, you might consider employing your own attorney to check that things are done properly and in a timely manner. Even if the Estate is small, consider consulting with an attorney any time you are concerned about the way the Probate is being conducted.

❖ RIGHT TO OBJECT TO THE WILL

The decedent's Will can be admitted into Probate by means of an informal proceeding (ARS 14-3303). You have the right to receive a copy of the Will that is offered for Probate. If you believe the Will is not valid, you can bring your concerns to the attention of the Court, but this is one of those issues that will require a Formal Probate procedure to settle.

❖ RIGHT TO DEMAND BOND

It doesn't happen often, but every now and again a Personal Representative will run off with Estate funds. A bond is insurance for the Estate. If Estate monies are stolen then the company that issued the bond will reimburse the Estate for the loss. It is up to the Court to decide whether a bond is necessary, and if so, the value of the bond. The Court will not order a bond if the Personal Representative is an authorized bank or trust company or if the Estate qualifies for Summary Administration and the surviving spouse is the Personal Representative. Also, the Court will not order bond if all of the beneficiaries *waive* (give up) the bond requirement in writing, or the Will waives bond (ARS 14-3603).

Most Wills state that no bond is required. The reason is two-fold. The Will maker chooses someone he trusts to administer the Estate, so he does not think a bond is necessary. And there are economic reasons. The cost of the bond is paid for by the Estate, and ultimately the amount inherited is reduced by the amount paid for the bond. The cost of the bond should not be a factor if there is any danger of the Estate property belong lost or mismanaged. If you are concerned about the safety of the Estate assets, it is important that you not sign a waiver and ask the Court to order the Personal Representative to be bonded.

✧ RIGHT TO HAVE COURT SUPERVISION

In Arizona, a Probate procedure can be Supervised or Unsupervised. In a **Supervised Administration**, the judge will supervise the distribution of the Estate. The Personal Representative cannot sell or transfer property without Court approval. Any deviation from the instructions given in the Will can be made only for good cause and with Court approval. In a Supervised Administration, the Personal Representative is responsible to answer to the Court as well as to all interested parties (ARS 14-3501, 14-3504).

The Court will order a Supervised Administration if the Will requires Supervision, unless circumstances have changed since the decedent prepared his Will and there is no current necessity to do so (ARS 14-3502). The Court will determine whether a Supervised Administration is necessary if the decedent died without a Will or if the Will does not require a Supervised Administration.

You as a beneficiary of the Estate can ask the Court to supervise the Estate, or not, depending on whether you think Court supervision is necessary. The only problem with asking the Court to supervise the Estate, is that it tends to increase the cost of administration. However, cost should not be a factor if you have any concern about the way the Personal Representative will settle the Estate.

✧ RIGHT TO KNOW PERSONAL REPRESENTATIVE'S FEES

The Personal Representative is entitled to be compensated for his efforts in settling the Estate (ARS14-3719). If he is also a beneficiary of the Estate he may decide not to take a commission and just take his inheritance. The reason may be economic. Any fee the Representative takes is taxable as ordinary income, but monies inherited are not taxable to him as a beneficiary. Ask the Personal Representative to tell you, in writing, whether he intends to charge a fee, and if so, how much.

There are no statutory guidelines for what is "reasonable" compensation. If you think the amount being charged is unreasonable, you can ask the Court to set a hearing on the matter. But before doing so, you should consult with an experienced Probate attorney to determine whether the amount being charged is the "going rate."

You can expect the Personal Representative, and his attorney, to contest your objection to the amount being charged, so you'd be wise to have your own attorney represent you at the hearing.

✧ RIGHT TO KNOW ATTORNEY'S FEES

It is the Personal Representative's job to use the Probate Estate to pay all valid claims and then to distribute what is left to the proper beneficiary. Debts are paid from the decedent's Estate and not from the Representative's pocket; but if the Personal Representative makes a mistake, he may be responsible to pay for it (ARS 14-3703).

The Personal Representative has the right to employ an attorney to guide him through the Probate procedure so that things will be done properly and at no personal cost to the Representative. It is proper to have the attorney paid with Estate funds.

You, as a beneficiary of the Estate, have the right to know how much will be charged for legal fees. Ask the Personal Representative to give you a copy of the retainer agreement. If the attorney is employed on an hourly basis, have the attorney give a written estimate of the time he expects to spend on the Probate proceeding.

Again, there is no statutory guideline for what is a "reasonable" fee for the attorney. You can call different law firms and ask what they charge to Probate an Estate with similar assets. That will give you some idea of the going rate. If after doing some "comparison shopping" you believe that the attorney's fee is not reasonable, you can negotiate with them to lower the fee. If you cannot reach an agreement, you can ask the Probate Court to set a hearing to settle the matter.

✧ RIGHT TO COPY OF THE INVENTORY

The Personal Representative must prepare an inventory of all of the assets of the Probate Estate within 90 days of his appointment. He can choose to file the inventory with the Court, or not. If he files the inventory with the Court, it becomes part of the public record and he is obliged to send a copy to any interested person who requests it. If he does not file the inventory with the Court, he must send a copy to each of the beneficiaries of the Estate. He must also send a copy to each person who has a financial interest in the Estate and who requests a copy.

The inventory should give the fair market value of the decedent's property as of the date of death. It must also indicate whether it is Community Property or Separate Property and whether there are any encumbrances on the property, i.e., whether any money is owed on the property (ARS 14-3706).

The value of the inventory is used to determine what is a reasonable fee for the Personal Representative and his attorney. It is also used to determine how much taxes need to be paid. It is important that you receive a copy of the inventory, and that you are satisfied with the value assigned to each item.

✧ RIGHT TO AN APPRAISAL

The Personal Representative can employ an appraiser to assist in determining the value of items included in the Estate inventory — but he is not required to have an appraisal unless ordered by the Court. If you are not satisfied with the value assigned to any Probate asset, you have the right to ask the Personal Representative to have the item appraised. If he refuses, you can ask Court to order an independent appraisal of the item.

✧ RIGHT TO AN ACCOUNTING

Before closing the Estate the Personal Representative should give you an accounting of how Estate funds were spent, and how the Representative intends to distribute whatever is left. He does not need to file the accounting with the Court unless the Administration is Supervised (ARS 14-3505, 14-3933).

If the Estate has significant assets you may want your own accountant to look over the accounting prior to the hearing. If there are any problems that your accountant can not resolve with the Personal Representative, you can ask for a Court hearing on the matter.

✧ RIGHT TO HAVE THE ESTATE CLOSED WITHOUT DELAY

How long it takes to complete the Probate proceeding depends on the size and complexity of the matter. The Personal Representative must publish notice to creditors in a newspaper of general circulation for three successive weeks. The creditor has four months from the first day the notice was published to file a claim with the Probate Court (ARS 14-3801).

Once the Personal Representative makes provision for the payment of any valid claim, he can close out the Estate at any time after the four month creditor period passes. If an Estate Tax return has been filed, the Estate should be closed within 90 days after the receipt of the state or federal tax release.

If you do not receive an accounting and a proposed plan of distribution within these time periods, you have the right to ask the Court to order the Personal Representative to either file an accounting with the Court or explain why he has not completed the administration of the Estate (ARS 14-3931).

✧ RIGHT TO RECEIVE A DEBT FREE INHERITANCE

Once a beneficiary finally receives his inheritance, about the last thing he wants to hear is that there is some unfinished business, or worse yet that monies need to be paid from the inheritance he received. But that is just what could happen if the Personal Representative distributes the money before all the creditors are paid. An unpaid creditor could sue the beneficiary any time within two years from the date of death (ARS 14-3801).

Taxes are another concern. You should ask to see a copy of all of the tax returns that were filed, and then verify that any monies that were due have been paid. Most importantly, you should not agree to having the Estate closed if the closing statement shows that there are any outstanding debts that need to be paid.

IT'S YOUR RIGHT - DON'T BE INTIMIDATED

You may feel uncomfortable being assertive with a friend or family member who is Personal Representative. Don't be. It's your money and your right to be informed. Be especially firm if the Personal Representative waves you off with "You've known me for years. Surely you trust me." People who are trustworthy, don't ask to be trusted. They do what is right. The very fact that the Personal Representative is resisting, is a red flag. In such situation, you can explain that it is not a matter of trust, but a matter of what is your legal right.

At the same time, keep things in perspective. Your relationship with the Personal Representative may be more important to you than the money you inherit. The job of settling an Estate can be complex and demanding. If the Personal Representative is getting the job done, let him know you appreciate his efforts.

THE CHECK LIST

We have discussed many things that need to be done when someone dies in the state of Arizona. The next page contains a check list that you may find helpful.

You can check those items that you need to do, and then cross them off the list once they are done. We made the list as comprehensive as possible, so many items may not apply in your case. In such case, you can cross them off the list or mark them *N/A* (not applicable).

Things To Do

FUNERAL ARRANGEMENTS TO BE MADE

☐ AUTOPSY   ☐ ANATOMICAL GIFT
☐ DISPOSITION OF BODY OR ASHES

DEATH CERTIFICATE

☐ HAVE DEATH CERTIFICATE RECORDED
GIVE COPY TO: _____

_____

NOTICE OF DEATH

PEOPLE TO BE NOTIFIED _____

COMPANIES TO NOTIFY
☐ TELEPHONE COMPANY
    ☐ LOCAL CARRIER   ☐ LONG DISTANCE   ☐ CELLULAR
☐ NEWSPAPER (OBITUARY PRINTED)
☐ NEWSPAPER DELIVERY CANCELLED   ☐ deposit refund
☐ SOCIAL SECURITY
☐ INTERNET SERVER CANCELLED
☐ TELEVISION CABLE/SATELLITE COMPANY CANCELLED
☐ POWER & LIGHT   ☐ deposit refund
☐ POST OFFICE
☐ OTHER UTILITIES (GAS, WATER)   ☐ deposit refund
☐ PENSION PLAN
☐ ANNUITY
☐ HEALTH INSURANCE COMPANY
☐ LIFE INSURANCE COMPANY
☐ HOME INSURANCE COMPANY
☐ MOTOR VEHICLE INSURANCE COMPANY
☐ CONDOMINIUM OR HOMEOWNER ASSOCIATION
☐ CANCEL SERVICE CONTRACT   ☐ deposit refund
☐ CREDIT CARD COMPANIES

_____

_____

_____

Things To Do

REMOVE DECEDENT AS BENEFICIARY OF:
- ☐ WILL   ☐ INSURANCE POLICY   ☐ PENSION PLAN
- ☐ BANK OR IRA ACCOUNT   ☐ SECURITY

DEBTS

PAY DECEDENT'S DEBTS (AMOUNT & CREDITOR)

_____

COLLECT MONIES OWED TO DECEDENT (AMOUNT & DEBTOR)

_____

TAXES
- ☐ FILE FINAL FEDERAL INCOME TAX RETURN
- ☐ FILE FINAL Arizona INCOME TAX RETURN
- ☐ RECEIVE INCOME TAX REFUND
- ☐ FILE ESTATE TAX RETURN

PROPERTY TO BE TRANSFERRED
- ☐ PERSONAL EFFECTS
- ☐ MOTOR VEHICLE
- ☐ BANK ACCOUNT
- ☐ CREDIT UNION ACCOUNT
- ☐ IRA ACCOUNT
- ☐ SECURITIES
- ☐ BROKERAGE ACCOUNT
- ☐ INSURANCE PROCEEDS
- ☐ HOMESTEAD
- ☐ TIME SHARE
- ☐ OTHER REAL PROPERTY
- ☐ CONTENTS OF SAFE DEPOSIT BOX

OTHER THINGS TO DO

_____

_____

_____

Once the Probate proceeding is over, you will be left with many documents and wonder which you need to keep:

COURT DOCUMENTS

You should keep a copy of the inventory to establish the value of property that you inherit. That value becomes your basis for any Capital Gains Tax that you may need to pay in the future. Other than the inventory, there is no reason to keep any Court document, provided you are satisfied with the way things were done; and do not intend to take action against the Personal Representative, or his attorney. The Registrar of the Probate Court keeps the Probate file on record, so if for some reason you later need a copy of a Probate document, you can get it from him.

PERSONAL RECORDS

The surviving spouse, or if no spouse, his next of kin should keep the decedent's personal papers (birth certificate, marriage certificate, naturalization papers, army records, religious documents, etc.). They may be needed in order to apply for government, or other, benefits. The next of kin may want to keep the decedent's medical records in the event that a family member needs to check out a genetic disorder.

TAX RECORDS

The IRS has up to three years to collect additional taxes, and you have up to seven years to claim a loss from a worthless security, so you should keep the decedent's tax file for seven years from the date of filing the return. You can learn more about which records to keep from the IRS publication 552. You can get the publication by calling the IRS at (800) 829-3676 or you can download it from their Website: http://www.irs.gov

Everyman's Estate Plan 7

The first six chapters of this book describe how to wind up the affairs of the decedent. As you read those chapters, you learned about the kinds of problems that can occur when settling the decedent's Estate. It is relatively simple for you to set up an Estate Plan so that your family members are not burdened with similar problems. An **Estate Plan** is the arranging of your finances for maximum control and protection during your lifetime, and at the same time ensuring that your property will be transferred quickly and at little cost to your heirs.

If you think that only wealthy people need to prepare an Estate Plan, you are mistaken. Each year, heirs of relatively modest Estates, spend thousands of dollars to settle an Estate. A bit of planning could have eliminated most, if not all, of the expense and hassle suffered by those families.

The suggestions in this chapter are designed to assist the average person in preparing a practical and inexpensive Estate Plan, so we named this chapter EVERYMAN'S ESTATE PLAN.

Once you create your own Estate Plan, you can be assured that your family will not be left with more problems than happy memories of you.

AVOIDING PROBATE

After reading the last Chapter, many will come to the conclusion that Probate is a good thing to avoid. Those who have $50,000 or less and no real property may not be concerned with avoiding Probate because as explained, your beneficiaries can get possession of that property without the need for a full Probate procedure. But Probate is necessary if you have property in your name only that exceeds $50,000.

Notice that the operative phrase in the last sentence is *in your name only*. Whether a Probate procedure is necessary depends on how your property is titled (owned). It makes no difference whether you do or do not have a Will. If you own property in excess of $50,000, and that property is titled in your name only, your beneficiaries will need to go through a Probate procedure in order to get possession of that property.

As explained in Chapter 5, there are many ways to title real property so that it passes automatically without the need for Probate. Residents of Arizona are fortunate to be able to name a beneficiary of the property in the form of a Beneficiary Deed. Upon your death, whoever you named as beneficiary will own the property without the need to go through Probate. Similarly if you own real property as Joint Tenants With Right of Survivorship, or if you own a Life Estate Interest, there will be no need to go through Probate. Ownership is established upon your death.

In this Chapter we examine ways to title your personal property (bank accounts, securities, etc.) so that it passes to your beneficiaries without the need for Probate.

OWNERSHIP OF BANK ACCOUNTS

You can arrange to have all of your bank accounts set up so that should you die, the money goes directly to a beneficiary. For example, suppose all you own is a bank account and you want whatever you have in the account to go to your son and daughter when you die. You might think that a simple solution is to put each child's name on the account as Joint Tenants With Right of Survivorship, but first consider the problems associated with a *Multiple Party Account*.

⊠ POTENTIAL LIABILITY

If you hold a bank account jointly with your adult child and that child is sued or gets a divorce, the child may need to disclose his ownership of that account. In such a case, you may find yourself spending money to prove that the account was established for your convenience only and that all of the money in that account really belongs to you.

⊠ OVERREACHING

You can set up a Multiple Party Account with your child so that the child has authority to withdraw funds from the account; however, monies could be withdrawn without your knowledge or consent (ARS 14-6222).

If you open a multiple party account with two of your children, there is the problem of what happens to the funds after your death. Should you die, your share of the account belongs to the surviving joint owners, equally (ARS 14-6201, 14-6212). But as a practical matter each joint owner has free access to the joint account. After your death the first child to the bank may decide to withdraw all of the money and that will, at the very least, cause hard feelings between them.

THE BENEFICIARY ACCOUNT

Holding a bank account jointly with a family member eliminates the need for Probate, but at the cost of control of the funds. One way to avoid Probate of the account yet retain full control during your lifetime, is to name one or more persons to be the beneficiary of the account. There are two forms of *Beneficiary Account*:

THE IN TRUST FOR ACCOUNT

You can direct a financial institution to hold your account *For the Benefit of* ("FBO") or *In Trust For* ("ITF") one or more beneficiaries you name. Your contract with the bank will state that the beneficiary does not have access to the account during your lifetime (ARS 6-236).

THE PAY ON DEATH ACCOUNT

You can have a contract with the bank that directs the bank to *Pay On Death* ("POD") all of the money in the account to one or more beneficiaries that you name.

If you open a Pay On Death account, unless there is clear evidence of a different intent in your agreement with the bank:

⇨ The beneficiary has no right to the account during your lifetime.

⇨ If there is more than one beneficiary of your POD account, upon your death, the monies are divided equally among the beneficiaries. If one of the beneficiaries dies before you do, the account goes to the surviving beneficiary. If all of the beneficiaries of the account die before you, the account becomes part of your Estate (ARS 14-6212).

A married couple who have an account with right of survivorship, can give the bank instructions to pay the monies to their child (or children) once both parties are deceased. Should one spouse die, the survivor owns the account and is free to close it out or continue with the same POD provision. The beneficiaries of the account have no right to any of the funds in the account until both parents are deceased (ARS 14-6212).

THE TRANSFER ON DEATH SECURITY

The Arizona law for securities is much the same as the statutes for bank accounts. You can arrange to have a security (a stock, bond or brokerage account) transferred to a beneficiary upon your death. You can instruct the holder of the security to PAY ON DEATH ("POD") or TRANSFER ON DEATH ("TOD") to a named beneficiary. For example, a security can be titled as:

TIM REILLY and OLIVIA REILLY,
AS JOINT TENANTS WITH RIGHT OF SURVIVORSHIP
TOD STUART REILLY

Stuart has no right to the security until both his parents die. The parents are free to change the beneficiary of the security at any time during their lifetime. If no change is made, Stuart will inherit the security once both parents are deceased. If Stuart dies before his parents and no other provision is made, the security will go to the Estate of the last parent to die (ARS 14-6222, 14-6302, 14-6305).

If your Estate consists only of bank accounts and/or securities, and you want all of your property to go to one or two beneficiaries without the need for Probate, but with maximum control and protection of your funds during your lifetime, then holding your property in any of these beneficiary forms: *For the Benefit Of* or *Pay On Death* or *Transfer On Death*, should accomplish your goal.

GIFT TO A MINOR CHILD

At the beginning of this chapter, we identified two problems with a joint account: potential liability if the joint owner is sued and overreaching by the joint owner. If you wish to make a gift to a minor child, then that presents still another problem. The Beneficiary Account avoids the problem of potential liability and overreaching, but if the beneficiary of such account is a minor, there is the problem of the child having access to a large sum of money.

Under Arizona law, if the amount in the account is under $10,000, the financial institution can transfer the funds to a trust company or to an adult member of the minor's family to keep till the child is 18 (ARS 14-7657). If the amount exceeds $10,000, the financial institution will not transfer the funds without authorization from the Probate Court. The Court may decide to appoint a Conservator to care for the child's property.

You may think it best that the child inherits more than $10,000 this way a Court will see to it that the monies are held safely till the child is an adult. But that only presents a new set of problems. It takes time, effort and money to set up a conservatorship. If you leave the child a significant amount of money, the Conservator has the right to be paid to manage those funds. It could happen that the cost of the conservatorship significantly reduces the amount of money inherited by the child. There are ways to avoid the problem of having a Conservator appointed to care for property inherited by a child, and yet ensure that the monies are protected. One such method is the ARIZONA UNIFORM TRANSFERS TO MINORS ACT.

THE UNIFORM TRANSFERS TO MINORS ACT

The *Arizona Uniform Transfers to Minors Act* is designed to protect gifts made to a minor by appointing someone to be the *Custodian* of a gift until the child is an adult. For example, you can make a minor child the beneficiary of your life insurance policy and name a trusted relative or friend to be the Custodian of the gift. Should you die while the child is a minor, the insurance company will give the proceeds of the policy to the person you named as Custodian to hold until the child is an adult.

You can make a gift to a minor in your Will. You can appoint your Personal Representative (or anyone else) as Custodian of the gift. For example:

I give the sum of $20,000 to_____ (name) as custodian for _____ (name of minor) under the Arizona Uniform Transfers to Minors Act.

THE LIFETIME GIFT

You can even use the Arizona Uniform Transfers to Minors Law to make gifts during your lifetime of items such as shares in a corporation or a limited partnership interest. You can nominate yourself as Custodian of the gift, or you can name another person or Trust company to serve as Custodian. Once the lifetime gift is made it becomes irrevocable, so this method is not appropriate unless you are sure that you want the child to have the gift once he/she is an adult.

In general, the Custodian must distribute the gift when the child reaches 18; however, if you make a lifetime gift, or a gift as part of your Will, you can direct the Custodian to distribute the gift when the child reaches 21 (ARS 14-7659, 14-7670).

The Custodian needs to invest and manage the property in a responsible, prudent manner. He must keep records of all transactions made with custodial property; and make those records available for inspection by the child's parent, or legal representative, or the child, if the minor is 14 or older. If those records are not to their satisfaction, they can petition (ask) the Probate Court to require the Custodian to give an accounting.

The Custodian has the discretion to use the gift to care for the child. The Custodian can pay monies directly to the child, or can use the money for the child's benefit. The Custodian can refuse to use any of the monies for the child and just keep the funds invested until it is time to distribute the funds. If the Custodian wants to keep the funds invested, the child's parent, or his legal representative, or the child once he is 14, can ask the judge of the Probate Court to order the Custodian to part with some or all of the money for the benefit of the child. The judge will decide what is in the child's best interest and then rule on the matter (ARS 14-7662, 14-7664).

The Custodian is entitled to be paid for his effort each year. If the gift is sizeable, the Custodian's fee can be sizeable. Before appointing a person or a financial institution as Custodian, it is best to come to a written agreement about what will be charged to manage the custodial property (ARS 14-7665).

A gift made under the Arizona Uniform Transfers to Minors Act is limited to one minor only (ARS 14-7660). If you want to give a single gift, such as a gift of real property to two or more children or if you want more flexibility about when the minor is to receive the gift, then a Trust may be the better way to go. We will discuss Trusts later in this chapter.

THE GIFT OF REAL PROPERTY

As explained in Chapter 5, if you own real property together with another, then who owns the property upon your death depends on how the Grantee is identified on the face of the deed. If you compare the Grantee clause of the deed to the examples given in Chapter 5 you can determine who will inherit the property when you die. If you are not satisfied with the way the property will be inherited, you need to consult with an attorney to change the deed so that it will conform to your wishes.

If you own the property in your name only or as a Tenant In Common, when you die, there will need to be a Probate proceeding to determine the proper beneficiary of that land. If your main objective is to avoid Probate, you can have an attorney change the deed so that upon your death, the property will descend to your beneficiary without the need for Probate. As with bank and securities accounts there are different ways to do so, each with its own advantages and disadvantages.

JOINT OWNERSHIP

If you hold property in your name only, and wish to avoid Probate, you can have your deed changed so that you and a beneficiary are joint owners with right of survivorship. If you do so, should either of you die, the other will own the property 100%. That avoids Probate, but by making that person joint owner, you are, in effect, making a gift of half of the property during your lifetime. You will not be able to sell that property without the beneficiary's permission. And if the beneficiary gives permission and the property is sold, the beneficiary will have the legal right to half of the proceeds of the sale. As explained on the next page, you may be creating a Capital Gains Tax problem as well.

You can arrange to sell your home without paying a Capital Gains Tax (see page 42), but if you make someone joint owner of your home who does not live with you, a Capital Gains Tax may need to be paid on the joint owner's share of the proceeds should you decide to sell the property.

CAUTION   GIFT OF HOMESTEAD

Some elderly parents worry that they may need nursing care at some time in the future and lose all of their life savings to pay for that care. The parent may decide that the best way to avoid Probate and protect the homestead from loss is to transfer the homestead to their child with the understanding that the parent will continue to live there until he/she dies. But this is just trading risks.

☒ RISK OF LOSS

Property transferred to your child could be lost if the child runs into serious financial difficulties or is sued. This is especially a risk if your child is a professional (doctor, nurse, accountant, financial planner, attorney, etc.). If your child is (or gets) married, this complicates matters even more. Should the child divorce, the property may need to be included as part of the settlement agreement. This may be to your child's detriment because the child may need to share the value of the property with his/her former spouse. If you do not transfer the property, it cannot become part of the marital equation.

☒ LOSS OF HOMESTEAD TAX EXEMPTION

As explained on page 43, in Arizona, Homestead Tax Exemptions are available for persons of low income who are disabled (ARS 42-11111). If you transfer your homestead, you lose your right to receive these tax breaks. It could cost more money in taxes to continue to live in your own home.

⊠ LOSS OF HOMESTEAD CREDITOR PROTECTION

As explained in Chapter 5, up to $100,000 of the equity of your homestead is protected from creditors during your lifetime (ARS 33-1101). If you simply transfer your homestead to a child, then you lose your homestead protection against creditors. If you are married, then it is a double loss of creditor protection. Not only do you lose creditor protection for yourself, you lose it for your spouse as well. If the child does not occupy that property as his homestead. There is no homestead creditor protection whatsoever. The child's creditors can force the sale of the property (that's your home) for relatively small amounts of unpaid debts.

⊠ POSSIBLE CAPITAL GAINS TAX

Although Congress has expressed an intent to phase out the Estate Tax, there is no discussion to do away with the Capital Gains Tax. If you gift the property to the child during your lifetime, when he sells the property he will pay a Capital Gains Tax on the increase in value from the price you paid for your home to the selling price at the time your child sells the property.

If you do not make the gift during your lifetime, the child will inherit the property with a step-up in basis, i.e., he will inherit the property at its market value as of the date of your death. Under today's tax structure and continuing until 2009, that step-up in basis is unlimited. If your child sells the property when he inherits it, he will pay no Capital Gains Tax, regardless of how large the step-up in basis. In 2010, there will be a limit on the amount that can be inherited free of the Capital Gains Tax but that limit is quite high so for most of us this is not a concern.

⊠   POSSIBLE GIFT TAX

If the value of the transfer is worth more than the Annual Gift Tax Exclusion (currently $11,000) you need to file a Gift Tax return. For most of us, this is not a problem because no Gift Tax need be paid unless the equity in your home (fair market value less mortgages on the property) plus the value of all gifts in excess of the Annual Gift Tax Exclusion that you gave over your lifetime, exceed $1,000,000 (see Chapter 2). But if your Estate is in that tax bracket, you need to be aware that you are "using up" your lifetime Gift Tax Exclusion.

⊠   POSSIBLE LOSS OF GOVERNMENT BENEFITS

If you transfer property, then depending upon the value of the transfer, you could be disqualified from receiving Medicaid or Supplemental Security Income ("SSI") benefits for a substantial period of time. When a person applies for Medicaid, he must disclose if, within three years of his application, he transferred property for less than the fair market value (i.e. he gifted property).

This reporting period extends to five years if the transfer was to a Trust. The ARIZONA LONG TERM CARE SYSTEM Eligibility Office will compute a disqualification period depending on the value of the transfer. This can present a serious problem should you need extended nursing care during that period of time.

Under current state and federal law, there are many ways to protect your homestead and still qualify for government benefits. Before transferring your homestead because of your concern for the cost of future health care, consult with an Elder Law attorney. He will be able to suggest ways to protect your assets, and still ensure that you receive the health care that you may require in your later years.

THE LIFE ESTATE, NOT A COMPLETE SOLUTION

Some of the problems we have discussed regarding an outright gift of the homestead can be avoided by transferring your home but keeping a Life Estate for yourself. This means that you have the right to occupy the property for so long as you live. Once you die your beneficiary will own the property without any need for Probate, but again there are downsides:

> ▷ You cannot sell the property during your lifetime without the beneficiary agreeing to the sale.

> ▷ If you sell the property, the beneficiary is entitled to some portion of the proceeds of the sale.

> ▷ If you or your beneficiary become incapacitated, the property cannot be sold unless a Conservator is appointed.

Before making any transfer of real property, it is important to consult with an Elder Law attorney and/or certified financial planner and/or accountant, to examine all aspects related to the transfer.

 **LAWYER**   OUT OF STATE PROPERTY

Each state is in charge of the way property located in that state is transferred. If you own property in another state (or country), you need to consult with an attorney local to that area to determine how that property will be transferred to your beneficiaries should you die. Many state laws are similar to Arizona, namely, property held as Joint Tenants With Right of Survivorship or a Life Estate Interest are transferred without the need for Probate.

If you own property in another state in your name only, or as a Tenant In Common, you may need to have a Probate procedure in Arizona, and a second Probate procedure in the state where the property is located. This could have the effect of doubling the cost of Probate.

Still another problem is the matter of taxes. Inheritance taxes may be due in the state where the property is located. It may be necessary to file an Income Tax and an Estate Tax return in two states. In addition to increased taxes, this can double the cost of the accounting fees.

You may wish to consult with an attorney for suggestions about how to set up your Estate Plan to avoid such problems.

A TRUST MAY BE THE SOLUTION (OR NOT)

A full Probate procedure may be necessary if you hold property in your name only or as a Tenant In Common. We explored different ways to re-title property to avoid Probate, but these methods have trade-offs that may be unacceptable to you. One way to avoid many of these potential problems is to set up a *Revocable Living Trust* (also known as an *Inter Vivos Trust*).

A Revocable Living Trust is designed to care for your property during your lifetime, and then to distribute your property once you die — without the need for Probate. You may have been encouraged to set up a Trust by your financial planner, attorney, or accountant. Even people of modest means are being encouraged to use a Trust as the basis of their Estate Plan. But Trusts have their pros and cons. Before getting into that, let's first discuss what a Trust is and how it works.

SETTING UP A TRUST

To create a Trust, a person has his attorney prepare a Trust document (a *Trust Agreement*) in accordance with his (the client's) needs and desires. The Agreement is between the person who creates and funds the Trust (the *Settlor* or *Grantor*) and the *Trustee* (manager) of property placed in the Trust. The Settlor usually appoints himself as Trustee so that he is in total control of property he places into the Trust. This means that he signs the Trust Agreement as the Settlor and also as the Trustee who promises to manage the property according to the terms of the Trust Agreement. The Trust document also names a *Successor Trustee* who will take over the management of the Trust property should the Trustee resign, become disabled, or die. We will refer to the Revocable Living Trust as the "Living Trust" or just the "Trust" and the person who creates the Trust as the "Settlor."

Once the Trust Agreement is properly signed, the Settlor transfers property into the Trust. He does this by changing title from his individual name to his name as Trustee. For example, if Elaine Richards sets up a Trust naming herself as Trustee, and she wishes to place her bank account into the Trust, all she need do is instruct the bank to change the name on the account from Elaine Richards to:

ELAINE RICHARDS, TRUSTEE OF THE ELAINE RICHARDS REVOCABLE TRUST AGREEMENT DATED JULY 12, 2005.

When the change is made, all the money in the account becomes Trust property. Elaine (wearing her Trustee hat) has total control of the account, taking money out, and putting money in, as she sees fit. Similarly, if she wants to put real property into the Trust, she can have her attorney prepare a new deed with the owner identified as ELAINE RICHARDS, TRUSTEE (see page 123 for an example of real property placed into a Trust).

Because the Trust is revocable, if she wishes, Elaine can terminate the Trust at any time and have all the Trust property returned and placed back into her own individual name. If she does not revoke her Trust during her lifetime, once she dies the Trust becomes irrevocable, and her Successor Trustee must follow the terms of the Trust Agreement as written. If the Trust says to give the Trust property to certain beneficiaries, the Successor Trustee will do so, and without the need for Probate. If the Trust directs the Successor Trustee to continue to hold property in Trust and use the money to take care of a member of Elaine's family, then the Successor Trustee will do so.

Setting up a Trust has many good features.

☆☆ AVOID PROBATE

In Arizona, Probate can be time consuming and very expensive. Both the Personal Representative and his attorney are entitled to payment for their services. These fees can be significant. It may be necessary to employ accountants and appraisers, and real estate brokers to sell property as well. If you have property in two states, two Probate procedures may be necessary (one in each state) and that could be costly in time, effort and money. If the Trust is properly drafted and your property placed into the Trust, you should be able to avoid Probate altogether.

☆ FEDERAL ESTATE TAX SAVINGS

Many people think that the federal Estate Tax will be phased out so that by 2010, no Estate Taxes will be due regardless of the size of an Estate. But under current law in 2011, the Estate Tax is scheduled to be reinstated and those who own property worth more than $1,000,000 will once again be subject to a sizeable Estate Tax. A couple with an Estate in excess of a million dollars can reduce the risk of an Estate Tax by setting up a Trust, so that each partner can take advantage of his own Estate Tax Exclusion.

For example, if a couple owns two million dollars, they can set up a Trust that separates the money into two Trusts once one partner dies. The Trust can be arranged so that the surviving spouse is free to use the income from both Trusts. Once both partners are deceased, the beneficiaries of their respective Trusts will inherit the funds, hopefully with no Estate Tax due. If the couple does not set up a Trust and continues to hold all of their property jointly, the last to die will own the two million dollars with only one Estate Tax Exclusion available.

☆ CARE FOR FAMILY MEMBER:

You can make provision in your Trust to care for a minor child or family member after you die. If your beneficiary is a minor, you can direct your Successor Trustee to distribute the child's inheritance at different times. For example, you can direct your Successor Trustee to give the beneficiary a certain amount of money when he is 18, then 21, then 25, then 30, etc.

If your intended beneficiary has a creditor problem, you can set up a *Spendthrift Trust*. You can direct your Successor Trustee to keep the funds in Trust and give the beneficiary enough money to pay for his health care, education or living expenses, and nothing more. With a properly drafted Spendthrift provision the Trust funds will be protected from the creditors of the beneficiary, with certain exceptions:

NO PROTECTION FROM SPOUSAL OR CHILD SUPPORT

A Court can require the Trustee to use Trust funds for the support of the spouse or child of the beneficiary. The Court can also order payment for necessary goods and services (food, clothing, shelter, etc.) furnished to the beneficiary. This includes reimbursement to the federal government or the state of Arizona for nursing care under the Medicaid program (ARS 14-7707).

NO CREDITOR PROTECTION FOR SETTLOR

You can set up a Spendthrift Trust for a beneficiary, but not for yourself. Because property held in your Revocable Living Trust is freely accessible to you, it is likewise accessible to your creditors both before and after your death. If you die owing money, your creditors can have a Personal Representative appointed to locate funds to pay those debts. The Personal Representative can require that your Trust property be used to pay for those debts (ARS 14-3711, 14-3715, 14-6102).

☆ PRIVACY

Your Living Trust is a private document. No one but your Successor Trustee and your beneficiaries need ever read it. If you leave property in a Will and there is a Probate procedure, the Will must be filed with the court, where it becomes a public document. Anyone can go to the courthouse, read your Will and see who you did (or did not) provide for in your Will. Records in the Probate Court (inventories, creditor's claims, etc.) are open to public scrutiny. In some states, Court records are now available on the Internet!

LEASE SAFE DEPOSIT BOX AS TRUSTEE

One of the benefits of having a Living Trust is that you can lease the safe deposit box in your name as Trustee. When you lease the safe deposit box you can have an agreement with the bank that they are to allow your Successor Trustee free access to the safe deposit box in the event of your incapacity or death (ARS 6-1001, 6-1002).

This protects your privacy. As explained in Chapter 3, if you hold the safe deposit box in your name only, access to the box is restricted upon your death. No one can take possession of the contents of your box without a Court order, but your next of kin can ask the bank to be allowed to examine the contents of the box to see if your Will is there. Under Arizona law the bank can allow such inspection, provided a bank officer or employee is present when the contents of the box are examined (ARS 6-1008).

By leasing a safe deposit box as Trustee, only you and your Successor Trustee need ever know of the contents of the box.

✰✰ AVOID CONSERVATORSHIP

Once you have a Trust, you do not need to worry about who will take care of your property should you become disabled or too aged to handle your finances. The person you appointed as Successor Trustee will take over the care of the Trust property, if you are unable to do so. If you do not have a Trust, and become incapacitated, a Court may need to appoint a Conservator to care for your property (ARS 14-5430). Conservatorship is a good thing to avoid, not only because of the cost of the procedure, but also to avoid the embarrassment of a Court coming to the conclusion that you are not competent to manage your own finances.

Before appointing a Conservator, the Court will have a hearing to determine whether you are competent to manage your property. You are entitled to your own attorney at the hearing. If you do not have one the Court can appoint an attorney for you (ARS 14-5303). If the Court determines that you do not have the capacity to handle your finances, he will appoint a Conservator. The Court may order the Conservator to obtain a bond for the protection of your property (ARS 14-5411).

The Conservator will need to employ an attorney to establish the Guardianship and see to it that it is properly administered. The Conservator and his attorney are entitled to be paid for their efforts on your behalf. Once appointed, the Conservator will take possession of your property and file an inventory with the Court. The Conservator will manage your property and each year account to the Court for monies spent. Under Arizona law, the Conservator can do much the same with your property as you can, i.e., he can buy, sell, lease, run your business, make repairs, invest your money, sue or defend a law suit, all without asking permission from the Court (ARS 14-5414, 14-5424).

The Conservator has the right to employ accountants, auditors, investment advisors, attorneys to assist with his duties. He may employ these professionals, regardless of whether they are business associates of the Conservator. For example, if the Conservator is a member of a brokerage firm, he may employ that firm to invest your money (ARS 14-5424).

Court filing fees, the cost of a bond, accounting fees, Conservator fees, your attorney fees, the Conservator's attorney fees, other professional fees, are all charged to you. And these expenses go on year after year until you are restored to capacity or die.

Establishing a Trust heads off the need for the appointment of a Conservator.

THE PROBLEMS

With all these perks, you may be ready to call your attorney to make an appointment to set up a Trust, but before doing so there are a few things you need to consider:

⊠ COMPLEXITY

A Trust is a fairly complex document, often 20 pages long. It needs to be that long because you are establishing a vehicle to take care of your property during your lifetime, as well as after your death. The Trust usually is written in "legalese," so it may take you considerable time and effort to understand it. It is important to have your Trust document prepared by an attorney who has the patience to work with you until you fully understand each paragraph of the document and are satisfied that what it says is what you really want.

⊠ COST

Because of the thoroughness of the document and the fact that it is custom designed for you, a Trust will cost much more to draft than a simple Will. In addition to the initial cost of the Trust, it can be expensive to maintain the Trust should you become disabled or die. Your Successor Trustee has the right to charge for his duties as Trustee, as well as to charge for any specialized services performed. A financial institution can charge to serve as Successor Trustee, and also charge to manage the Trust portfolio. If you decide to have a financial institution serve as Trustee, then it is important that you compare the fee schedules of different institutions.

You can choose an attorney, or an accountant, or a financial planner, to serve as Trustee, but this may create a conflict of interest because the professional can use his position as Trustee to generate fees. If you decide to appoint a professional as Trustee you should have a fee agreement stating what will be charged for his duties as Trustee and what will be charged for professional work done on behalf of the Trust. The fee agreement should be included in the Trust document with a provision that whoever accepts the job of Successor Trustee, agrees to accept the fee as provided in the Trust document.

You may decide to appoint your spouse or a family member as Successor Trustee, who may want little, or no, compensation. Regardless of who you choose to be Successor Trustee, you need come to a fee agreement. The agreement can be for a set amount or a percentage of the value of the Trust, or other method to be used to determine his compensation.

⊠ PROBATE MIGHT STILL BE NECESSARY

The Trust only works for those items that you place in the Trust. If you own property in your name only, then upon your death, a Probate procedure might be necessary in order to transfer the property to your beneficiary. For example, if you purchase a security in your name only, without a "Transfer On Death" designation to a named beneficiary or to your Trust, then a Probate procedure may be necessary to determine who should inherit the security.

The attorney who prepares the Trust usually creates a safety net for such situations. He prepares a Will for you to sign at the same time you sign the Trust. The Will makes your Trust the beneficiary of your Probate Estate. If you own anything in your name only and a Probate procedure is necessary, the Will directs your Personal Representative to make that asset part of your Trust by transferring the asset to your Successor Trustee. Your Successor Trustee will add that asset to your Trust (ARS 14-2511).

The Will prepared by the attorney is called a **Pour Over Will** because it is designed to "pour" any asset titled in your name only, into the Trust. Having the Will ensures that all of your property will go to the beneficiaries named in your Trust. But the downside of holding property in your name only is that a full Probate procedure may be necessary just to get that asset into your Trust. If avoiding Probate is your goal, holding property, in your name only, defeats that goal.

You can ensure that a Probate procedure will not be necessary by transferring your assets into your Trust during your lifetime, but if you neglect to put something into your Trust, the Pour Over Will stands by to transfer that asset into your Trust.

⊠ TAXES MAY STILL BE A PROBLEM

While you are operating the Trust as Trustee, all of the property held in your Revocable Living Trust is taxed as if you were holding that property in your own name. If the value of your Trust property exceeds the Estate Tax Exclusion value, taxes will be due once you die. If all you own is held in your Trust, your Successor Trustee will need to pay those taxes from the Trust property.

Those who have Estates large enough to incur Estate Taxes also need to think about how taxes will be paid on other taxable transfers. For example, suppose you and your brother bought a home as Joint Tenants With Right of Survivorship. If you each contributed equally to the purchase, and the property is now worth one million dollars, your brother will inherit your half million dollar share. If you also own two million dollars in other property all of which is in your Trust, your Taxable Estate is $2,500,000.

Unless your Trust directs otherwise, each beneficiary of your Estate is responsible to pay a proportionate share of the Estate Taxes. If federal Estate Taxes are reinstated so that anything over one million dollars is taxable at a rate of 40%, your Estate Tax will be $600,000. Your brother will need to contribute his prorated share of the Estate Taxes:

$$\$500,000 / \$2,500,000 = .2$$
$$20\% \text{ of } \$600,000 = \$120,000.$$

But suppose your brother doesn't have that kind of cash? Should he be forced to sell his home in order to pay the taxes? Should your Successor Trustee use your Trust property to pay your brother's taxes with a promise that he will reimburse the beneficiaries of your Trust at a later date? An experienced Estate Planning attorney can suggest any number of ways to head off such problems.

⊠ YOU MAY NEED YOUR SPOUSE'S PERMISSION TO TRANSFER PROPERTY INTO YOUR TRUST

Most married couples prepare a Trust as part of their overall Estate Plan. Sometimes a married person has a Trust that was prepared prior to the marriage, or he may decide to create a Trust to care for children from a previous marriage. The Settlor is free to place any of his Separate Property and his half of the couple's Community Property into his Trust but he may not place his spouse's half of the Community Property into the Trust (or anywhere else not accessible to his spouse) without the spouse's written consent.

If you are married and make a transfer of Community Property into your Trust without your spouse's permission; and that transfer results in your spouse not having a half interest in the Community Property, then your spouse has the right to petition the Court to undo the transfer and return his/her share of the Community Property.

⊠ ☆ THE TRUST IS LEGALLY ENFORCEABLE

Your Successor Trustee will take over the administration of your Trust upon your incapacity or death. Should there be a dispute regarding the administration of the Trust, your beneficiary (or your Successor Trustee) can petition the Court to settle the matter. For example, your Successor Trustee is entitled to reasonable compensation. If you did not set the amount he is to be paid in the Trust Agreement and the beneficiaries object to the amount he is charging, they can ask the Court to determine his compensation (ARS 14-7201).

We gave this section a cross and a star because the right to have a Trust enforced or administered by the Court is a double edged sword. It is great to have the Court protect the rights of your beneficiaries, but the cost of a court battle could be greater than if your Estate was Probated and the money simply distributed to your beneficiaries.

The beneficiaries of your Trust are at a financial disadvantage in a dispute with your Successor Trustee. The Court can require your Trustee to be personally liable for his legal costs, but that only happens if the Trustee acted illegally or unreasonably. In most cases, the Trustee will be able to charge the expense of defending his actions to your Trust and your beneficiaries will pay for their legal expenses out of their own pockets.

Win or lose, there will be just that much less for your beneficiaries to inherit.

MAYBE PROBATE ISN'T ALL THAT BAD

Although all of the methods discussed in this Chapter can be used to transfer property without the need for Probate, each method may have a downside that is objectionable to you. Maybe you don't have enough money to warrant the cost of setting up the Trust at this time. Holding property jointly with another may raise issues of security and independence. Holding property so that it goes directly to a few beneficiaries in a Pay On Death account may not be as flexible as you wish.

This is especially the case if you wish to give gifts to several charities or to minor children instead of just one or two beneficiaries. For example, if you hold all your property so that it goes to your son without the need for Probate, and you ask him to use some of the money for your grandchild's education, it may be that your grandchild gets none of the money because your son is sued or falls upon hard times. If you keep your property in your name only and leave a Will giving a certain amount of money for your grandchild, the child will know exactly how much money you left and the purpose of that gift.

After taking into account all the pros and cons of avoiding Probate, you may well opt for a Will and a Probate procedure. If you make such a decision, it is important to keep in mind that Estate Planning is not an "all or nothing" choice. You can arrange your Estate so that certain items pass automatically to your intended beneficiary, and other items can be left in your name only, to be distributed as part of a Probate procedure. By arranging your finances in this manner, you can reduce the value of your Probate Estate, and that in turn should reduce the cost of Probate.

Your Arizona Will

Many people decide that the Will is the best route to go but do not act upon it, thinking it unnecessary to prepare a Will until they are very old and about to die. But according to reports published by the National Center for Health Statistics (a division of the U.S. Department of Health and Human Services) 2 of every 10 people who die in any given year are under the age of 60.

Twenty percent may seem like a small number until it hits close to home as it did with a young couple. They were having difficulty conceiving a child. They went from doctor to doctor until they met someone just beginning his practice. With his knowledge of the latest advances in medicine, he was able to help them.

The birth of their child was a moment of joy and gratitude. They asked a nurse to take a picture of them all together — the proud parents, the newborn child and the doctor who made it all possible. Happiness radiated from the picture, but within 6 months, one of them would be dead.

You might think it was the child. An infant's life is so fragile. SIDS and all manner of childhood diseases can threaten a little one. But no, he grew up a healthy young man.

If you looked at the picture, you might guess the husband. Overweight and stressed out, his ruddy complexion suggested high blood pressure. He looked like a typical heart- attack-prone Type A personality.

No, he was fine and went on to enjoy raising his son.

Probably it was the wife. She had such a difficult time with the pregnancy and the delivery was especially hard. Maybe it was all too much for her.

No, she recovered and later had two more children.

It was the doctor who was killed in a collision with a truck.

WHY A WILL IS NECESSARY

Though we all agree that one never knows, still people put off making a Will figuring that if they die before getting around to it, Arizona law will take over and their property will be distributed in the manner that they would have wanted anyway. The problem with that logic is the complexity of Arizona's Laws Intestate Succession. If you are survived by a spouse, child, parent or sibling, it isn't too difficult to figure out who will inherit your property. But if none of these survive you, the ultimate beneficiary of your property may not be the person you would have chosen, had you taken the time to make a Will.

Others think that it is not necessary to have a Will because they arranged their finances so that all of their property will be inherited without the need for Probate. But money could come into your Estate after your death. This could happen in any number of ways. You might die in a house fire, or a flood. Your insurance company may need to pay for damages done to your home. You might be killed in a car accident caused by the wrongful act of someone. In such case, a Personal Representative may need to be appointed to sue on behalf of your Estate.

As explained in Chapter 6, without a Will, the Court will use an order of priority as set by Arizona law to appoint a Personal Representative. The person chosen by the Court may not be the person you would have chosen to settle your Estate. And as we will see in this Chapter, there are other important reasons to make a Will.

SET THE PERSONAL REPRESENTATIVE'S FEE

An important reason to make a Will is to choose your Personal Representative and to come to an understanding about how much compensation he will receive. You can state that value in your Will.

CAUTION   THE PERSONAL REPRESENTATIVE CAN SEEK MORE MONEY

Even though your Will states the amount of compensation to be given to your Personal Representative, he may decide to ask the Probate Court to award a greater value. (ARS 14-3719). To avoid the problem, you can have your attorney draft an Agreement that you and your Personal Representative sign and attach to your Will.

Having a separate fee Agreement will not stop your Personal Representative from asking for more money, but with such an Agreement, the Court will not agree to the increase unless something unusual occurs (such as a law suit) causing much more work than the ordinary Probate procedure.

You also need to keep in mind that the Personal Representative's fee is just to administer the Estate. It does not include payment for professional work he may do while settling the Estate. For example, if you appoint your attorney as Personal Representative, he can agree to the amount stated in the Will for his role as Personal Representative, and then ask the Court to award him attorney's fees as well (ARS 14-3709).

The same goes for any other professional. If you appoint your accountant to serve as Personal Representative, he is entitled to receive compensation for his work as Personal Representative and also for any accounting work he does such as preparing and filing tax returns, preparing an inventory and doing an accounting for the beneficiaries. A financial planner who serves as Personal Representative may be compensated for his management of the Estate property (buying and selling securities, taking care of rental property, etc.) in addition to his fee to administer the Estate.

But the main problem with appointing a professional as your Personal Representative is the same as appointing a professional to serve as the Successor Trustee of your Trust, namely, that it creates a potential conflict of interest. The professional can use his position as Personal Representative to generate fees that may not have been necessary if someone else settled the Estate.

When choosing a Personal Representative, consider the relationship of the Personal Representative to the beneficiaries and determine whether it would be better to appoint a non-professional for the job.

DETERMINE THE TYPE OF PROBATE PROCEDURE
If you wish to have a Court supervise the settlement and distribution of your Estate, have your Will state that you wish a Supervised Administration. If your Will does not specifically state that the Probate is to be supervised, unless your beneficiaries ask for Court supervision.it will be unsupervised (ARS 14-3502). But the down-side of requiring a Supervised Administration is that it tends to increase the cost of Probate because the Personal Representative must seek Court approval before acting.

If you feel comfortable that your Personal Representative will administer your Estate in a prudent manner, you may wish to allow an Unsupervised Administration. Your beneficiaries are always free to ask the Court to supervise the Probate procedure, should they be concerned about the way your Personal Representative will administer your Estate.

MAKE GIFTS OF YOUR PERSONAL PROPERTY

Another benefit to making a Will is that you can make provision for who will get your personal property, including your car. If you make a gift of your car in your Will, it will be relatively simple for your car to be trans-ferred to the beneficiary. If you do not make a specific gift of your car, it becomes part of your Probate Estate. Your Personal Representative will decide what to do with the car. He can sell it and include the proceeds of the sale in the Estate funds to be distributed to your residuary beneficiaries; or he can give the car to one beneficiary of your Estate as part of that beneficiary's share of the Estate.

SMALL GIFTS MATTER

Many who have lost someone close to them report that the distribution of small personal items caused the greatest conflict. If you arrange your finances so that no Probate proceeding is necessary, your next of kin will need to decide how to distribute your personal effects. Without guidance from you and no Representative with authority to make decisions, there could be much disagreement and hard feelings, over items of little monetary value.

If you make a Will, you can make gifts of your personal effects (record collection, books, jewelry etc.) by making a list of these gifts and attaching it to your Will — or by referring to the list in your Will. Your Personal Representative will distribute your personal effects according to that list. You can change the list at any time just so long as you sign and date the list. No witness to your signature is needed. The list is for items with more sentimental than monetary value. You should not include money gifts in that list. Those items need to be given as part of your Will (ARS 14-2513).

Of course, you cannot list each and every item you own, but you can instruct your Personal Representative to allow certain family members to take their choice of items not mentioned in your Will. If two or more family members want the same item, have your Personal Representative use an appropriate lottery system (coin toss, high card in a cut of a deck of cards, etc.) to decide who "wins."

📑 CHOOSE A GUARDIAN FOR YOUR MINOR CHILD
Each parent has the right to name someone in their Will to be Guardian of their child in the event that the parent dies before the child is grown, and the other parent is deceased. Should the surviving parent die, whoever the parent named to serve as Guardian will have priority to be appointed as Guardian of the minor child.

It is important to name someone who is compatible with the child, because if the child is 14 or older, he can object to the appointment and ask the Court to appoint someone else. The judge will give serious weight to the child's choice of Guardian. But, ultimately, the decision is with the judge. He will appoint a Guardian based on what he determines to be in the best interests of the child (ARS 14-5202, 14-5203, 14-5204, 14-5206).

MAKE ADJUSTMENT FOR PRIOR GIFTS

You can use your Will to make adjustments for gifts or loans given during your lifetime. For example, if you have loaned money to a family member and do not expect to be repaid, you can deduct the loan from that person's inheritance. There is no need to make the adjustment if the borrower gives you a promissory note because should you die, the monies will be owed to your Estate and the Personal Representative can deduct the monies owed from the borrower's inheritance. But if there is no evidence of the debt and you neglect to make a Will, the borrower will receive whatever is allowed under the Laws of Intestate Succession (ARS 14-2109). That was the case with Sally and Tom and their four children. They were firm believers in treating each of their children equally. "Share and share alike" was their favorite saying. Once Tom died, Sally continued with the tradition.

Sally did not think of the loan she gave to her son as a gift. After all, he promised to pay it back, with interest! She did not ask her son to sign a promissory note. He was family. If you can't trust your son, who can you trust?

The son was prompt with his monthly payments. But only two payments had been made before his mother died suddenly, from a heart attack. Sally never mentioned the loan to any of her other children. Neither did her son.

Each child received one quarter of their mother's Estate; and no one the wiser. Except whenever Sally's son dreams of his mother, she is not smiling.

▤ MAKE PROVISION FOR PAYMENT OF DEBTS AND TAXES

Under Arizona law, if monies are owed on your car, home or other property, and you make a specific gift of that item, your beneficiary will inherit the loan along with the gift (ARS 14-2607). Taxes are another concern for those Estates large enough to be subject to Estate Taxes. State and federal law require that Estate Taxes be paid by the beneficiaries of the Estate in proportion to the value received, unless the decedent made some other arrangements to pay for the taxes. If you make no provision for the payment of taxes, whoever inherits your property will pay a percentage of the taxes based on the amount they receive (26 U.S.C. 6324 (a)(2)).

The beneficiary must pay his share regardless of whether he inherits the property through a nonprobate transfer (joint owner, beneficiary of your Trust, beneficiary of a Pay On Death account, beneficiary of a life insurance policy, etc.) or as the beneficiary of your Probate Estate. (ARS 14-6102). If a beneficiary refuses to contribute his share of the taxes, whoever is required to make payment (usually the surviving spouse or Personal Representative) can ask the Court to order the beneficiary to contribute his share of the taxes.

If this is not as you wish, you can direct your Personal Representative to pay all of your debts and taxes from your Probate Estate. If you do so, beneficiaries of a specific gift, and those who inherit property from a nonprobate transfer will not contribute to the payment of your taxes. All of your taxes will be paid from your Probate Estate. This means that the amount that your residuary beneficiaries receive will be reduced by the amount of money paid for debts and taxes.

PREPARING AND STORING YOUR WILL

A Will may look like a simple document, but it takes a certain amount of legal expertise to write it in a manner that will give effect to the wishes of the Will maker. Your Will needs to be clearly worded so there is no doubt about what you intended. A sentence that can be read in two different ways can lead to a dispute over what you intended; and that could result in a long and expensive Court battle. Even though Arizona statute (ARS 14-2503) allows a Holographic (hand-scribed) Will to be admitted to Probate, it could be challenged in any number of ways as discussed in Chapter 5. If you are serious about having your property distributed exactly as you wish, it is best to have an attorney who is experienced in Estate Planning, prepare a Will for you. He will supervise the signing of your Will. Should the need arise, he will be able to testify that you were fully competent when you signed the Will and that you did so of your own free will.

STORING THE WILL

Once you sign your Will, you may wonder where to store it. Your attorney may suggest that he place it in his vault for safekeeping. By doing so, he ensures that your heirs will need to contact him as soon as you die. This does not mean that they are required to employ him should a Probate proceeding be necessary. It only means that he will have an opportunity for future employment. But there are problems with such an arrangement. The Will could be lost or mistaken for another Will. That happened in at least one case. The attorney prepared Wills for two people with the same name and similar family circumstances. When one person died the attorney submitted the wrong Will to Probate.

Luckily the error was quickly discovered. The decedent had a distinctive signature. The family challenged the validity of the Will based on the unfamiliar signature and the way the property was to be distributed. They knew the decedent would never have distributed his property in the manner stated in the Will.

Should you decided to allow your attorney to store your Will, you need assurances that the attorney will be responsible for the document. You should get a receipt and something in writing that says:

⇨ The attorney accepts full responsibility for the storage of the Will. Should it be lost or damaged, he will redraft the document for you to sign at no cost to you. If you are deceased, he will, at no cost to your heirs, present sufficient evidence to the Court to accept a valid copy of the Will into Probate.

⇨ There will be no charge to you, or your heirs, for the storage and retrieval of the document.

⇨ Should he sell his practice, retire, or die, he or the successor to his practice, will return the original document to you.

THE SAFE DEPOSIT BOX — SAFE BUT . . .

You might consider placing your Will in a safe deposit box that you lease at a bank. The only problem with the bank safe deposit box is convenient access. If you hold a safe deposit box in your name only, should you die, the bank will restrict access to the safe deposit box. As explained in Chapter 3, the bank may allow a family member to inspect the contents of your safe box provided they do so under the supervision of an officer or employee of the company.

If your Will is there, they can forward it to the Probate Court or deliver it to the named Executor, but the bank will not allow anything else to be removed without Court authority (ARS 6-1008). Once a Personal Representative is appointed by the Court, he will have such authority and be able to remove the contents of the safe deposit box. However, if you arranged your finances to avoid Probate, it is self defeating to have entry to a safe deposit box trigger a Probate procedure.

For those who are happily married, the solution to the problem of accessing the safe deposit box after death, is to lease the box jointly with your spouse, such that each of you has free access to the box (ARS 6-1004). This may not be the best solution if you think your spouse will be unhappy with certain provisions made in your Will. Some Wills never see the light of day for this reason.

As explained in Chapter 7, those who have a Trust can solve the problem by giving their Successor Trustee joint access to the safe deposit box.

If you are single and do not have a Trust, you can lease the box jointly with a trusted family member. But if privacy and security are important to you, this might offset any concern for the convenience of your beneficiaries.

Of course, you can always keep your Will in a fireproof safe in your home.

Regardless of where you choose to store your Will, let your Personal Representative know that you have a Will and how to retrieve it in the event of your death.

CHOOSING THE RIGHT ESTATE PLAN

Joint Ownership?
A Pay On Death bank account?
A Transfer On Death Security?
A Trust?
A Will?
An Insurance Policy???

Chapters 7 and 8 offer so many options that the reader may be more confused than when he was blissfully unenlightened.

As with most things in life, you may find there are no ultimate solutions, just alternatives. The right choice for you is the one that best accomplishes your goal. This being the case, you first need to determine what you want to accomplish with the money you leave. Think about what will happen to your property if you were to die suddenly, without making any plan different from the one you now have.

> Who will be responsible to pay your bills?
> Who will get your property?
> Will Probate be necessary?

If the answers to these questions are not what you wish, then you need to work to arrange your property to accomplish your goals.

For those with significant assets — especially those with Estates large enough to pay Estate Taxes, a trip to an experienced Estate Planning attorney may be well worth the consultation fee.

Your Estate Plan Record 9

Once you are satisfied with your Estate Plan, then the final thing to consider is whether your heirs will be able to locate your assets once you are gone.

Most people have their business records in one place, their Will in another place, car titles and deeds in still another place. When someone dies, their beneficiaries may feel as if they are playing a game of "hide and seek" with the decedent. The game might be fun were it not for the fact that an unlocated item may be forever lost. For example, suppose you die in an accident and no one knows you are insured by your credit card company for accidental death in the amount of $25,000. The only one to profit is the insurance company, which is just that much richer because no one told them that you died as a result of an accident.

And how about a key to a safe deposit box located in another state? Will anyone find it? Even if they find the key, how will they find the box?

It is not difficult to arrange things so that your affairs are always in order. It amounts to being aware of what you own (and owe) and keeping a record of your possessions. A side benefit is that by doing so, you will always know where all your business records are. If you ever spent time trying to collect information to file your taxes or trying to find a lost stock or bond certificate, you will appreciate the value of organizing your records.

ORGANIZING YOUR RECORDS

Heirs need all the help they can get. It is difficult enough dealing with the loss, without the frustration of trying to locate important documents. Your heirs will have no problem locating your assets if you keep all of your records in a single place. It can be a desk drawer or a file cabinet or even a shoe box. It is helpful if you keep a separate file or folder for each type of investment. You might consider setting up the following folders:

THE BANK & SECURITIES FOLDER

Store your original certificates for stocks, bonds, mutual funds, certificates of deposit, in a folder labeled **BANK & SECURITIES**. In addition to the original certificate, include a copy of the contract you signed with each financial institution. The contract will show where you have funds and who you named as beneficiary or joint owner of the account. If someone owes you money and signed a promissory note or mortgage identifying you as the lender, store these documents in this folder as well.

If you have a safe deposit box, keep a record of its location and the number of the box. Keep a copy of all of the items stored in the box in this folder. If you have an extra key to the box, put it here.

E-bank Accounts If you are doing your banking on-line, it is important to keep a record of your passwords so that your family can access the account in the event of your incapacity or death. The same applies if you have on-line brokerage or installment loan accounts. Keep a paper record of these accounts in this folder.

📁 THE INSURANCE FOLDER

The INSURANCE FOLDER is for each insurance policy that you own, be it life insurance, car insurance, homeowner's insurance or a health care insurance policy. If you purchased real property, you probably received a title commitment at closing and the title insurance policy some weeks later when you received your original deed from recording. If you cannot locate the title insurance policy, contact the closing agent and have him send you a copy of your title policy.

📁 THE PENSION AND ANNUITY FOLDER

If you have a pension or annuity, then put all of the documents relating to the pension in this folder. Include the telephone number and/or address of the person to contact in the event of your death.

FOR FEDERAL RETIREES If you are a federal retiree, you should have received your PERSONAL IDENTIFICATION NUMBER (PIN) and the person who will inherit your pension (your *survivor annuitant*) should have his/her own PIN as well. It is relatively simple to obtain this during your lifetime, but it may be difficult and/or stressful for your survivor annuitant to work through the system once you are gone.

Survivor annuitant benefits are not automatic. Your survivor annuitant must apply for them by submitting a death claim to the Office of Personnel Management. Your survivor needs to know that it is necessary to apply and also how to apply. You can get printed information about how to apply for benefits from the Office Of Personnel Management (see page 34). Keep the printed information in this file.

🗁   THE DEED FOLDER

Many people save every scrap of paper associated with the closing of real property. If you closed recently on real estate and there was a mortgage involved in the purchase, you probably walked away from closing with enough paper to wallpaper your kitchen. If you wish, you can keep all of those papers in a separate file that identifies the property, for example:

CLOSING PAPERS FOR THE PHOENIX PROPERTY

Place the original deed (or a copy if the original is in a safe deposit box) in a separate **DEED FOLDER**. Include cemetery deeds, condominium deeds, cooperative shares to real property, timesharing certificates, deed to out of state property, etc. Also include a copy of related documents such as an Abstract of Title, or a recorded Condominium Approval. If you have a title insurance policy, put the original in the insurance folder, and a copy in this folder. If you have a mortgage on your property, put a copy of the recorded mortgage and promissory note in a separate **LIABILITY FOLDER**.

LOCATING REAL PROPERTY
If you own a vacant lot, your beneficiaries will find the deed (or a copy) in this folder but that deed will not contain the address of that property because it doesn't have one. The post office does not assign a street address until there is a building on the site. Your beneficiaries can get the location of the property from city or county records. But why make things hard for them? Include a handwritten note in this folder that tells them exactly how to locate the property.

📁 THE LIABILITY FOLDER

The **LIABILITY FOLDER** should contain all loan documents of debts that you owe. For example, if you purchased real property and have a mortgage on that property, put a copy of the mortgage and promissory note in this folder. If you owe money on a car, put the loan documents in this folder. If you have a credit card, put a copy of the contract you signed with the credit card company in this folder. A lease is a liability, because you contracted to pay a certain amount for the period of the lease, so include a copy of any lease agreement in this folder.

Many people never take the time to calculate their *net worth* (what a person owns less what that person owes). By having a record of your assets and outstanding debts, you can calculate your net worth whenever you wish.

📁 THE ESTATE PLANNING DOCUMENT FOLDER

Place your Estate Planning documents (Will, Trust, Premarital Agreement, Community Property Agreement, burial, funeral arrangements, etc.) in a separate folder. If your attorney has your original documents, or you placed the original in a safe deposit box, place a copy of the document in this folder together with instructions about how to find the original. It is important to keep a copy of your Will or Trust because over the years you may forget what provision you made. Keeping a copy in your home may save you a trip to the safe deposit box to determine whether you need to update the document.

📁 THE SEPARATE PROPERTY FOLDER

It is important for couples in a Community Property Regime to keep a careful record of their ownership of Separate Property. If one partner is unable to pay his Separate Obligations, his creditors might suspect that property owned by the other partner is really Community Property and ask a Court to order an accounting. A careful record of the ownership of Separate Property may head off such investigation.

Married or single it is important to keep a record of your personal property in the event that it is lost or stolen:

MOTOR VEHICLES Keep the title to all of your motor vehicle titles in this folder. This includes cars, mobile homes, boats, planes, etc. If you owe money on the vehicle, the lender may have possession of the title certificate. If such is the case, put a copy of the title certificate and registration in this folder and a copy of the loan documents in a separate liability folder. If you have a boat or plane, identify the location of the motor vehicle. For example, if you are leasing space in an airplane hangar or in a marina, keep a copy of the leasing agreement in this file.

JEWELRY   If you own expensive jewelry, keep a picture of the item together with the sales receipt or written appraisal in this folder.

COLLECTOR'S ITEMS If you own a valuable art or coin collection, or any other item of significant value, include a picture of the item in this file. Also include evidence of ownership of the item, such as a sales receipt or a certificate of authenticity, or a written appraisal of the property.

🗁 THE PERSONAL RECORDS FOLDER

The **PERSONAL RECORDS FOLDER** should include documents that relate to you personally such as a birth certificate, naturalization papers, marriage certificate, divorce papers, military records, Social Security card, etc. If you have a Power of Attorney, you can place the document in this folder, or in your Estate Planning folder. If you placed the original document in a safe deposit box, keep a copy in this folder together with the location of the original.

🗁 THE TAX RECORD FOLDER

Your Personal Representative (or next of kin) will need to file your final income tax returns. Keep a copy of your tax returns (both federal and state) for the past three years in your **TAX RECORD FOLDER**. As explained in Chapter 2, beginning in 2010, there will be a cap on the step-up basis to 4.3 million dollars for property inherited by the spouse and 1.3 million dollars for property inherited by anyone else. It is important to keep a record of the basis of your property, not only for your heirs, but for yourself should you decide to sell the property during your lifetime. If you purchase real property, you need to keep a record of the purchase price as well as monies you paid to improve the property. For condominiums, that includes special assessments made to improve the property. You will need these records to determine whether there will be a Capital Gains Tax on the transfer. Your accountant can help you set up a bookkeeping system to keep a running record of your basis in everything you own of value.

THE *If I Die* FILE

Many do not have the time, nor inclination, to "play" with all these folders. They do not anticipate an immediate demise. Getting hit by a truck, or dying in a fiery plane crash is not something to think about, much less prepare for. But consider that death is not the only problem. You could take suddenly ill (say with a stroke) and become incapacitated. Even the most time-starved optimist should have a murmur of concern that his loved ones will be left with a mess should something unforeseen happen.

If you do not feel like doing a complete job of organizing your records at this time, consider an abridged version. You can set up a single file with a list of all you own and the location of each item. You need to make that file easily accessible to whomever you wish to manage your affairs in the event of your incapacity or death. You can do this by letting that person know of the existence of the file and how to get it in an emergency; or keep the file in an easily accessible place in your home with the succinct but attention-grabbing title of "*If I Die*."

We have included a form on the next page that you can use as a basis for information to be included in the file.

If I Die

the following information will help settle my Estate:

INFORMATION FOR DEATH CERTIFICATE

MY FULL LEGAL NAME _____

MY SOCIAL SECURITY NO. _____

MY USUAL OCCUPATION _____

BIRTH DATE AND BIRTH PLACE _____

If naturalized, date & place _____

MY FATHER'S NAME _____

MY MOTHER'S MAIDEN NAME _____

PEOPLE TO BE NOTIFIED

_____

_____

_____

FUNERAL AND BURIAL ARRANGEMENTS

LOCATION OF BURIAL SITE

_____

LOCATION OF PREPAID FUNERAL CONTRACT

_____

FOR VETERAN or SPOUSE BURIAL IN A NATIONAL CEMETERY

BRANCH_____SERIAL NO._____

VETERAN'S RANK _____

VETERAN'S VA CLAIM NUMBER _____

DATE AND PLACE OF ENTRY INTO SERVICE:

_____

DATE AND PLACE OF SEPARATION FROM SERVICE:

_____

LOCATION OF OFFICIAL MILITARY DISCHARGE
OR DD 214 FORM_____

LOCATION OF LEGAL DOCUMENTS

BIRTH CERTIFICATE _____

MARRIAGE CERTIFICATE_____

DIVORCE DECREE _____

PASSPORT _____

WILL OR TRUST _____

DEEDS _____

MORTGAGES _____

TITLE TO MOTOR VEHICLES _____

POWER OF ATTORNEY _____

Attorney name & telephone _____

LOCATION OF FINANCIAL RECORDS

INSURANCE POLICIES:

Name of Company, Location of Policy, Insurance Agent

_____

_____

PENSIONS/ANNUITIES:

IF FEDERAL RETIREE: PIN NUMBER: _____

NAME OF SURVIVOR _____

SURVIVOR PIN NUMBER _____

BANK

Name and address of Bank, Account Number,
Location of Safe Deposit Box and Key

_____

_____

SECURITIES

Broker name and telephone

_____

TAX RECORDS FOR PAST 3 YEARS

LOCATION _____

Accountant name and telephone

_____

KEEPING UP TO DATE

We discussed people's natural disinclination to make an Estate Plan until they are faced with their own mortality. Many believe that they will make just one Will and then die (maybe that's why they put off making a Will). The reality is, most people who make a Will change it at least once before they die. If you have an Estate Plan, it is important to update it when any of the following events take place:

✍ CHANGE IN MARITAL STATUS
GETTING MARRIED

In the early 20th century, marriage was a simple thing. Two young people fell in love, and married. There was no need for a Premarital Agreement because they came to the marriage with little property and an intent to stay together "till death do us part." Today, young people postpone marriage until they have established careers, so they are coming into the marriage with property that they worked hard to acquire. The intent to remain married remains, but young people are realistic. They know the statistics. Half of the marriages don't work out. But, ever optimistic, the majority of those who divorce will re-marry at least once and in many cases, with children from a prior union.

It is a foolhardy couple who enter a marriage in today's society without a Premarital Agreement that spells out the rights and responsibilities of the couple in the event that one of them dies, or they divorce. Courts in Arizona will enforce the agreement, provided the document was prepared according to Arizona law, i.e., the document was signed voluntarily after full disclosure of the finances of each party or the right to full disclosure was waived in writing (ARS 25-202).

A Premarital Agreement that is too one-sided can be challenged in Court, so it is important that both parties be represented by their own attorney.

Once the honeymoon is over, it is important to examine your pre-marriage Estate Plan. As explained in Chapter 5, if you do not change the Will you signed before you married, your spouse may be able to challenge that Will, unless your Premarital Agreement gives up statutory rights as they apply to married people. You should review your Premarital Agreement on a regular basis as your finances change or as you have children. With the consent of your spouse, you can amend your Premarital Agreement. If it needs a complete revision, you can revoke the Agreement, and replace it with a Postmarital Agreement.

Changes to the original agreement need to be prepared and signed in the same manner as your original agreement. There must be full disclosure by both parties as to the extent of their wealth. Each of you should be represented by your own attorney.

GETTING DIVORCED

Under Arizona law, should you divorce and die before you get around to changing your Will, any gift that you made in your Will or Trust for your former spouse, or to a relative of your spouse, is revoked (ARS 14-2804). Your Probate Estate will be distributed as if your spouse died before you did.

A legal separation in the state of Arizona does not end the marriage, however a decree of separation ends your Community Property rights and obligations. In particular, property you owned as Community Property becomes a Tenancy In Common with each person owning half the property (ARS 25-313, 25-318B).

But it is best not to rely on changes that take place by law. If you divorce (or even separate) it is important to review all of your Estate Planning documents (deeds, pension plans, insurance policies, Will or Trust etc.) to determine whether you wish to name a new beneficiary of your property.

✍ A CHANGE IN RELATIONSHIP

If you marry, separate, divorce, have a child, or if a beneficiary of your Estate dies, you need to examine your Will to determine whether it needs to be revised. It is important to have changes made by a properly drafted and signed document. If you make changes by crossing things out or writing over your Will, the validity of the document can be challenged once you die.

Simply ripping up the old Will effectively revokes the Will (ARS 14-2507). But it could happen that someone (perhaps your attorney) has a copy of the Will. If no one knows that you revoked the Will, they may think the Will is lost and offer a copy of the Will for Probate (see page 84).

NOTIFY EMPLOYER OF CHANGE

If you change your marital status (either marry or divorce) you need to tell your employer of the change so that the employer can change your status for purposes of paycheck tax deductions. If you have a health insurance plan or a pension plan, that provides benefits to your spouse, then these need to be changed as well.

As explained in Chapter 6, Arizona law allows up to $5,000 in wages to be transferred to your surviving spouse (ARS 14-3971A). If you change your marital status, you need to inform your employer, in writing, who is to receive your unpaid wages in the event of your death. Ask your employer to put that document in your work file.

BENEFICIARY MOVES OR DIES

Most people remember to name an alternate beneficiary should one of their beneficiaries die. But how many of us remember to notify the pension plan or insurance company when a beneficiary moves? Many life insurance proceeds are never paid because the company cannot locate the beneficiary. The Actuarial Office of the Federal Employees' Group Life Insurance Program reported that as of September, 2003, they had over 55.8 million dollars in unpaid benefits, mostly because they could not locate the beneficiary at the last given address.

✍ RELOCATION TO A NEW STATE OR COUNTRY

There is no need to change your Estate Plan for a move within the state of Arizona. There is much to check out if you are moving to another state. If your attorney has your original Will (or any other original document), then unless you plan to continue to employ him as your attorney, you need to retrieve your originals and take them with you to the new state.

You need to determine whether your Will conforms to the laws of the state of your new residence. Most states will honor a Will drafted according to Arizona law, however, the rights of a spouse vary considerably state to state. If you are married and have not provided the minimum amount as required by the laws of the new state, should you die before your spouse, your Will may be challenged on that basis. The same applies to a Trust. Many states require funds from a Revocable Living Trust be used to pay the minimum amount allowed by law to the surviving spouse.

If you do not have a Will, it is important to check out the Laws of Intestate Succession for that state. In some states they are referred to as the *Laws of Descent and Distribution*. Each state has its own laws relating to the inheritance of property and those laws are very different from each other. Who has the right to inherit your property in Arizona may be different from who can inherit your property in another state. This is the time to think about who has a right to inherit your property in the state of your new residence. There is a world of difference in the rights of a spouse in a Community Property state (Arizona, California, Idaho, Louisiana, Nevada, New Mexico, Texas, Washington and Wisconsin) and other states. There is even variation in the rights of a spouse from one Community Property state to another!

OTHER ESTATE PLANNING DOCUMENTS

A *Medical* or *Health Care Directive* is a document that gives instructions about the health care a person does (or does not) want to receive in the event that he is too ill to make his own health care decisions. In Arizona, that document is called a *Health Care Power of Attorney*, and the person who is appointed to carry out the given instructions is called the *Health Care Attorney-In-Fact* (ARS 36-3224, 36-3262).

If you have an Arizona Health Care Power of Attorney, it is best to sign a new Medical Directive should you move to another state. Other states have laws that enable you to appoint someone with powers similar to a Health Care Agent, but the laws of the state may refer to such person as a *Patient Advocate* or a *Health Care Surrogate* or a *Health Care Representative*. It is best to have a Health Care Directive using the forms and terms that are recognized in that state, rather than chance any confusion should you become ill and find yourself in an emergency situation.

Similarly, if you appointed someone to handle your finances under a Power of Attorney, you may want to have another prepared in conformity with the laws of the new state, so there will be no question of the right of your Agent to conduct business on your behalf.

CREDITOR PROTECTION
Creditor protection is another item that is significantly different state to state. If you have much debt, then determine what items can be inherited by your family free of your debts.

TAX CONCERNS
You also need to check out the taxes of the new state. Each state has its own tax structure. Some states have an inheritance tax, or a transfer tax on all inherited property. If state taxes are high, you may need an Estate Plan that will minimize the impact of those taxes.

When moving to another state you need to either educate yourself about the laws of the state, or consult with an attorney who can assist you in reviewing your Estate Plan to see if that plan will accomplish your goals in that state.

✍ A SIGNIFICANT CHANGE IN THE LAW
A major problem associated with the legal system in the United States is its volatility. Changes might be easy to keep up with if we had only one set of laws. But we are ruled by federal statutes and regulations and state statutes and regulations. We pay state and federal legislators to make laws and change existing statutes and regulations. We pay judges to tell us the meaning of the law, but their interpretation of the law may change the way the law operates. The legislature and the judiciary do their job and so laws and regulations change frequently and often without prior notice.

We, the public, are charged with the duty of understanding the law. Many a citizen has been chided with "Ignorance of the law is no excuse." Most of us have a general concept of what is and what is not allowed in our society, however, when presented with a particular problem, we may need to turn to a professional (lawyer, accountant, journalist, city official, etc.) to get an explanation of the law.

Areas of the law that affect you and your family, personally, are discussed in this book, namely Probate Law, Tax Law, and Estate Planning (Wills and Trusts). It is important to keep up with news in these areas to learn about changes in the law that may affect your Estate Plan. It is a good idea to check with your attorney on a regular basis to determine whether you need to change your Will or Trust because of a change in state or federal law.

Also check out the Eagle Publishing Company Website for changes we will post to keep this book fresh.
http://www.eaglepublishing.com

GAMES DECEDENTS PLAY

We discussed the game of "hide and seek" some decedents play with their heirs. A variation of that game is the "wild goose chase." The person who plays this game is one who never updates his files. His records are filled with all sorts of lapsed insurance policies, promissory notes of debts long since paid, brokerage statements of securities that have been sold, and so on.

When he is gone, his family will become frustrated as they try to hunt down the "missing" asset. If you wish to play this game, then the best joke is to keep the key to a safe deposit box that you are no longer leasing. That will keep folks hunting for a long time!

If you do not have a wicked sense of humor, then do your family a favor and update your records on a regular basis.

Glossary

ABSTRACT OF TITLE An *Abstract of Title* is a condensed history of the title to the land. It consists of a summary of all the recorded documents that affect the land, including mortgages.

ADMINISTRATION The *Administration* of a Probate Estate is the management and settlement of the decedent's affairs. There are different types of administration. See *Ancillary Administration* and *Summary administration.*

ADMINISTRATIVE LAW JUDGE An *Administrative Law Judge* is someone who is appointed to conduct an administrative hearing. He has the power to administer oaths, take testimony, and then decide the facts of the case. Although he can decide the facts of the case, the final outcome of the hearing is decided by the government agency that appointed the Administrative Law Judge.

AFFIANT An *Affiant* is someone who signs an affidavit and swears or acknowledges that it is true in the presence of a notary public or other person with authority to administer an oath or take acknowledgments.

AFFIDAVIT An *Affidavit* is a written statement of fact made by someone voluntarily, under oath, or acknowledged as being true, in the presence of a notary public or someone else who has authority to administer an oath or take acknowledgments.

AGENT An *Agent* is someone who is authorized by another (the *Principal)* to act for, or in place of, the Principal.

ANATOMICAL GIFT   An *Anatomical Gift* is the donation of all or part of the body of the decedent for the purpose of transplantation or research.

ANCILLARY ADMINISTRATION An *Ancillary Administration* is a Probate proceeding that aids or assists the original (primary) Probate proceeding. Ancillary administration is conducted to determine the beneficiary of the decedent's property located within that state, and to determine whether the property is taxable in that state.

ANNUAL GIFT TAX EXCLUSION The *Annual Gift Tax Exclusion* is the amount a person can gift to another each year without being required to file a federal Gift Tax Return. The Annual Gift Tax Exclusion is currently $11,000, but is expected to increase to $12,000 in the year 2006.

ANNUITANT   An *annuitant* is someone who is entitled to receive payments under an annuity contract.

ANNUITY An *annuity* is a contract that gives someone (the annuitant) the right to receive periodic payments (monthly, quarterly) for the life of the annuitant or for a given number of years.

ARS   *ARS* is the abbreviation for the *Arizona Revised Statutes*.

ASSET An *asset* is anything owned by someone that has a value, including personal property (jewelry, paintings, securities, cash, motor vehicles, etc.) and real property (condominiums, vacant lots, acreage, residences, etc.).

ASSIGN To *assign* is to transfer one's rights in or to something to another. For example, a contract may allow a party to assign his rights in the contract to another person.

ATTORNEY or ATTORNEY AT LAW An *attorney*, also known as an *Attorney at law*, or a *lawyer*, is someone who is licensed by the state to practice law in that state.

BASIS The *basis* is a value that is assigned to an asset for the purpose of determining the gain (or loss) on the sale of the item or in determining the value of the item in the hands of someone who has received it as a gift.

BENEFICIARY A *beneficiary* is one who benefits from the act of another or from the transfer of property. In this book we refer to a beneficiary as someone named in a Will, Trust, or deed to receive property, or someone who inherits property under the Laws of Intestate Succession.

BENEFICIARY DEED A *Beneficiary Deed* is a deed that transfers property to the beneficiary of the deed upon the death of the Grantor, provided the Grantor does not revoke the deed prior to his death. The beneficiary has no right in the property until the Grantor dies; i.e., the Grantor can revoke the Beneficiary Deed without asking permission from the beneficiary, or even telling the beneficiary that the deed has been revoked.

BOND A *bond* required by the Probate Court is a written document that guarantees the Personal Representative will perform his duties as required by law. The person or company that insures the performance of the Personal Representative is called a *surety.* The value of the bond is set by the Court. The cost of purchasing the bond is charged to the decedent's Estate.

CAPITAL GAINS TAX A *Capital Gains Tax* is a tax on the amount the net sales proceeds exceeds the basis of a capital asset sold by a taxpayer.

CAVEAT *Caveat* is Latin for "Let him beware." It is a warning for the reader to be careful.

CFR   *CFR* is the abbreviation for the *Code of Federal Regulations.*

CLAIM A *claim* against the decedent's estate is a demand for payment of a debt of the decedent. To be effective, the claim must be filed with the Probate Court within the time limits set by law.

CODE   A *Code* is a body of laws arranged systematically for easy reference e.g. the Internal Revenue Code.

COLUMBARIUM A *Columbarium* is a separate room or building with niches (spaces) designed to store urns containing the ashes of cremated bodies.

COMMON LAW MARRIAGE   A *Common Law marriage* is one that is entered into without a state marriage license or any kind of official marriage ceremony. A Common Law marriage is created by an agreement to marry, followed by the two living together, and telling everyone they know that they are husband and wife. Arizona does not recognize a Common Law marriage unless it was entered into in another state that considers the union to be a valid marriage.

COMMUNITY PROPERTY STATE Certain states (Arizona, California, Idaho, Louisiana, Nevada, New Mexico, Texas, Washington, and Wisconsin) have laws stating that property acquired by husband or wife, or both, during their marriage is *Community Property* and is owned equally by both of them.

COMMUNITY PROPERTY ACCOUNT A *Community Property Account* is an account owned by a married couple. Should one of them die, half of the account becomes the property of the surviving spouse. The other half is distributed according the decedent's Will or Trust; or if neither of these, then according to the Laws of Intestate Succession.

COMMUNITY PROPERTY WITH RIGHT OF SURVIVORSHIP *Community Property With Right of Survivorship* is a the name of a form of ownership that enables a married couple to own property with the right of the spouse to inherit the property without going through a Probate procedure, and yet preserving the Community status of the property, i.e., enabling the surviving spouse to take a step-up in basis of the entire value of the property.

CONSERVATOR A *Conservator* is someone appointed by the Probate Court to manage, protect and preserve the property of someone who is missing, or who the Court finds is unable to care for his property because of age (a minor) or incapacity.

CONFLICT OF INTEREST A *conflict of interest* is a conflict between the official duties of a fiduciary (Guardian, Trustee, attorney, etc.) and his own private interest. For example, it is a conflict of interest for a Successor Trustee to use Trust property for his own personal profit.

COURT The *Court* as used in this book is the Probate Court. When referring to an order made by the court, the term is synonymous with "judge," i.e., an "order of the court" is an order made by the judge of the court.

CREDITOR A *creditor* is someone to whom a debt is owed by another person (the *debtor*).

CREMAINS *Cremains* is shorthand for *cremated remains*. It refers to the ashes of a person who was cremated.

CURTESY *Curtesy* is the right of a husband, upon the death of his wife, to a life estate in real property she owned during their marriage, provided they had a surviving child who could inherit the property. This English Common Law has been abolished in most states, including Arizona.

CUSTODIAN A *Custodian* under Arizona's *Uniform Transfers to Minors Act* is a person or a financial institution that accepts responsibility for the care and management of property given to a minor child.

DAMAGES *Damages* is money that is awarded by a Court as compensation to someone who has been injured by the action of another.

DEBTOR A *debtor* is someone who owes payment of money or services to another person (the *creditor*).

DECEDENT The *Decedent* is the person who died.

DESCENDANT A *descendant* is someone who descends from a common ancestor. There are two kinds of descendants: a *lineal descendant* and a *collateral descendant*. The lineal descendant is one who descends in a straight line such as father to son to grandson. The collateral descendant is one who descends in a parallel line, such as a cousin. In this book, unless otherwise stated, the term *descendant* refers to a *lineal descendant*.

DEVISEE A *Devisee* is someone who inherits a gift of real property by Will.

DISTRIBUTION The *distribution* of a Trust or Probate Estate is the giving to the beneficiary that part of the Estate to which the beneficiary is entitled.

DOWER *Dower* is the right of a wife, upon the death of her husband, to a Life Estate in one-third of all real property that he owned during their marriage. This English Common Law has been abolished in most states, including Arizona.

ENCUMBRANCE An *encumbrance* is a claim or a lien or a liability that is attached to real property, such as a mortgage, or lease or a mechanic's lien.

EQUITABLE *Equitable* is whatever is right or just. If property is distributed to two or more people equitably, then the division is not necessarily equal, but according to the principles of justice or fairness.

ESTATE A person's *Estate* is all of the property (both real and personal property) owned by that person. The decedent's Estate may also be referred to as his *Taxable Estate* because all of the decedent's assets must be included when determining whether Estate Taxes are due. Compare to PROBATE ESTATE.

EXECUTOR An *Executor* (feminine *Executrix*) is a legal term found in many Wills. The terms refer to the person appointed by the Will maker to carry out directions given in the Will. In modern Wills, this term has been replaced by *Personal Representative.*

EXEMPT PROPERTY *Exempt Property* are those items which the surviving spouse or surviving children can inherit free from the claims of the decedent's creditors.

FAMILY ALLOWANCE The *Family Allowance* is the amount set aside by the Probate Court to pay for the support and maintenance of the decedent's surviving spouse and dependents during the Administration of the Estate.

FIDUCIARY A *Fiduciary* is one who takes on the duty of holding property in Trust for another or acting for the benefit of another, such as a Personal Representative, Trustee, Guardian etc.. A fiduciary relationship is also one that is developed out of trust and confidence. For example, an attorney has a fiduciary relationship with his client.

FORMAL PROBATE PROCEDURE A *Formal Probate Procedure* is a Probate Procedure that involves the settlement of an issue associated with the Probate, such as a challenge to the Will. A hearing, or trial, may be necessary in order to settle the dispute. All interested parties to the dispute must be given formal notice of the hearing.

GRANTEE   The *Grantee* of a deed is the person who receives title to real property from the *Grantor*.

GRANTOR   The *Grantor* is someone who transfers property. The Grantor of a deed is the person who transfers real property to a new owner (the Grantee). The Grantor of a Trust is someone who creates the Trust and then transfers property into the Trust. Also see SETTLOR.

GUARANTOR A *Guarantor* is someone who promises to pay a debt or perform a contract for another person in the event that person does not fulfill his obligation.

GUARDIAN A *Guardian* is someone who has legal authority to care for the person of a minor or for someone who has been found by the Court to be incapacitated.

HEALTH CARE AGENT A *Health Care Agent* is someone who is appointed by another (the *Principal*) to make medical decisions on behalf of the Principal, in the event that the Principal is to too ill to speak for himself.

HOLOGRAPHIC WILL A *Holographic Will* is a Will written, dated and signed by the hand of the Will maker himself. Many states refuse to admit a Holographic Will into Probate unless it is witnessed according to the laws of the state.

HOMESTEAD The *homestead* is the dwelling and land owned and occupied as the owner's principal residence.

HOMESTEAD ALLOWANCE The *Homestead Allowance* is the amount of money (currently $18,000) that the surviving spouse, or minor or dependent children can keep free of the decedent's creditor claims.

HEIR An *heir* is anyone entitled to inherit the decedent's property under the Laws of Intestate Succession in the event that the decedent dies without a Will.

INCAPACITATED The term *incapacitated* is used in two ways: A person is *physically incapacitated* if he has a physical disability. A person is *legally incapacitated* if a Court finds that a person is unable to care for his person or property. Once a judge determines that a person is legally incapacitated, he will appoint someone to care for the person and/or property of the incapacitated person.

IRA ACCOUNT An *Individual Retirement Account ("IRA")* is a retirement savings account in which income taxes on certain deposits and interest to the account are deferred until the monies are withdrawn.

IRREVOCABLE TRUST An *Irrevocable Trust* is a Trust that cannot be changed, cancelled or terminated until its purpose is accomplished.

INTER VIVOS TRUST   An *Inter Vivos Trust* (also known as a *Living Trust*) is a Trust that is created and becomes effective during the lifetime of the Grantor (or Settlor) as opposed to a Trust that he includes as part of his Will to take effect upon his death.

INTESTATE *Intestate* means not having a Will or dying without a Will. *Testate* is to have a Will or dying with a Will.

JOINT AND SEVERAL LIABILITY   If two or more people agree to be *jointly and severally liable* to pay a debt, then each individually agrees to be responsible to pay the debt, and together they all agree to pay for the debt.

JOINT TENANCY In Arizona, a *Joint Tenancy* means that each tenant owns an equal share of the property. There are no rights of survivorship unless the deed specifically says so.

KEY MAN INSURANCE *Key man insurance* is an insurance policy designed to protect a company from economic loss in the event that an important employee of the company becomes disabled or dies.

LAWS OF INTESTATE SUCCESSION *The Laws of Intestate Succession* are the laws of the state relating to who is entitled to inherit the decedent's Probate Estate when he dies without a valid Will

LEGALESE *Legalese* refers to the use of legal terms and confusing text that is used by some attorneys to draft legal documents.

LETTERS *Letters* is a document, issued by the Probate court, giving the Personal Representative authority to take possession of and to administer the Estate of the decedent.

LIEN A *lien* is a charge against a person's property as security for a debt. The lien is evidence of the creditor's right to take the property as full or partial payment, in the event that the debtor defaults in paying the monies owed.

LIFE ESTATE A *Life Estate* interest in real property is the right to possess and occupy the property for so long as the owner of the Life Estate lives. When the owner of the Life Estate dies, the property will belong to the owner of the *Remainder Interest*.

LITIGATION *Litigation* is the process of carrying on a lawsuit, i.e., to sue for some right or remedy in a court of law. A Litigation Attorney is one who is experienced in conducting the law suit and in particular, going to trial.

MEDICAID *Medicaid* is a public assistance program sponsored jointly by the federal and state government to provide Medical Assistance for people with low income and limited assets.

NET PROBATE ESTATE The *Net Probate Estate* is the value of the decedent's Probate Estate, less all the monies paid to settle the Estate, i.e. what is left once all valid claims and the costs and expenses of the Probate procedure are paid.

NET PROCEEDS The *net proceeds* of a sale is the sale price less costs and expenses paid to make the sale.

NET WORTH A person's *net worth* is the value of all of the property that he owns less the monies he owes.

NEXT OF KIN *Next of kin* has two meanings in law: *next of kin* refers to a person's nearest blood relation or it can refer to those people (not necessarily blood relations) who are entitled to inherit the property of a person who dies without a valid Will.

NONPROBATE TRANSFER A *Nonprobate Transfer* is the transfer of property to the decedent's beneficiary without the necessity of a Probate Procedure. This includes property that is transferred to the surviving joint owner, or property transferred to the beneficiary of a Pay On Death accounts.

PERJURY *Perjury* is lying under oath. The false statement can be made as a witness in court or by signing an Affidavit. Perjury is a criminal offense.

PERSONAL EFFECTS *Personal effects* is personal property that is kept for one's personal use such as clothing, jewelry, books, and other items generally found in the home.

PERSONAL PROPERTY *Personal property* is all property owned by a person that is not real property (real estate). It includes personal effects, cars, securities, bank accounts, insurance policies, etc.

PERSONAL REPRESENTATIVE A *Personal Representative* is someone appointed by the Probate Court to settle the decedent's Estate and to distribute whatever is left to the proper beneficiary.

PER STIRPES *Per Stirpes* is a method of distributing property to a group of beneficiaries. In the event a beneficiary dies before the gift is distributed, the deceased person's share goes to his descendants. If he has no descendants, the surviving beneficiaries share equally in the gift.

PETITION A *Petition* is a formal written, request to a Court asking the Court to take action or issue an order on a given matter; e.g. a request to appoint a Guardian.

POWER OF ATTORNEY A *Power of Attorney* is a document in which someone (the *Principal*) gives another person (his *Agent* or *Attorney In Fact*) authority to do certain things on behalf of the Principal.

PREMARITAL AGREEMENT A *Premarital Agreement* (also known as an *Prenuptial Agreement)* is an agreement made prior to marriage whereby a couple determines how their property is to be managed during their marriage and how their property is to be divided should one die, or they later divorce.

PRINCIPAL   The *Principal* of a Power of Attorney is the person who permits or directs another (his *Attorney-In-Fact* or *Agent*) to act for him.

PROBATE *Probate* is a Court procedure in which a Court determines the existence of a valid Will. The decedent's Estate is then settled by the Personal Representative who pays all valid claims and then distributes whatever remains to the proper beneficiary.

PROBATE ESTATE The *Probate Estate* is that part of the decedent's estate that is subject to Probate. It includes property that the decedent owned in his name only or as a Tenant In Common. It does not include property that was jointly with right of survivorship. It does not include property held "in trust for" or "for the benefit of" someone.

PRO BONO The term *Pro Bono* means "for the public good." When an attorney works Pro Bono, he does so voluntarily and without pay.

PUNITIVE DAMAGES *Punitive damages* are awarded by a Court to punish someone who deliberately disregarded the rights or safety of another. It is money awarded in addition to *compensatory damages* which are monies awarded to reimburse the wronged person for actual losses.

QRP *QRP* is the abbreviation for *Qualified Retirement Plan.* It is a retirement plan that qualifies for certain federal income tax deferrals or credits.

REAL PROPERTY *Real property,* also known as *real estate,* is land and anything permanently attached to the land such as buildings and fences.

REMAINDER INTEREST The *Remainder Interest* in real property is the property that passes to the owner of that Interest, once the owner of the Life Estate dies. See LIFE ESTATE

RESIDUARY BENEFICIARY A *Residuary Beneficiary* of a Will is a beneficiary who is entitled to whatever is left of the Probate Estate once specific gifts made in the Will have been distributed and once the decedent's bills, taxes and costs of Probate have been paid. If there is more than one residuary beneficiary, then unless the Will states differently they share equally in the Residuary Estate.

RESIDUARY ESTATE The *Residuary Estate* is that part of the Probate Estate that is left after all the debts, taxes, and costs of administration are paid and specific gifts distributed.

REVOCABLE TRUST A *Revocable Trust* is a Trust which can be amended or revoked by the Settlor during his lifetime.

REVOCABLE LIVING TRUST A *Revocable Living Trust* (also known as an *Inter Vivos Trust*) is a Revocable Trust that is created and becomes effective during the lifetime of the Settlor.

RIGHT OF SURVIVORSHIP A *Right of Survivorship* is the right of the survivor of a deceased person to the property of the decedent.

SECURED DEBT A *secured debt* is a debt backed by property. If the borrower does not pay the loan, the lender can take the property. Car loans and mortgages are secured debts.

SELF PROVED WILL A *Self Proved Will* is a Will that eliminates some of the formalities of proof in a Probate procedure. The Will is made Self Proved by an Affidavit, signed by the witnesses, in the form as required by the statute.

SEPARATE PROPERTY In Arizona, the term *Separate Property* refers to property that is owned by a married person in his/her own right. It includes property owned by the person prior to marriage, as well as inheritances and gifts received by the person during the marriage.

SETTLOR A *Settlor* (also known as a *Grantor*) is someone who creates and then funds a Trust.

SIBLING A *sibling* is one of two or more people born of the same parents; i.e., a brother or a sister. Unless, otherwise noted, we used the term to include those who have only one parent in common; i.e. a half brother or a half sister.

SOLEMNIZE To *solemnize* a marriage is to enter a marriage publicly, before witnesses, rather than privately as in a common law marriage.

SPECIFIC GIFT) A *Specific Gift* is a gift of a specific item, or part of the Will maker's Estate, that is made to a named beneficiary of the Will.

SPENDTHRIFT   A *spendthrift* is someone who spends money carelessly or wastefully or extravagantly.

SPENDTHRIFT TRUST   A *Spendthrift Trust* is a Trust created to provide monies to a beneficiary, and at the same time protect the Trust property from being taken by the creditors of the beneficiary.

STATUTE OF LIMITATION A *Statute of Limitation* is a federal or state law that sets maximum time periods for taking legal action. Once the time set out in the statute passes, no legal action can be taken.

STATUTORY AGENT A *Statutory Agent* of a corporation is someone who is authorized to act on behalf of the company and accept service of process in the event the company is sued.

STEPPED-UP BASIS   A *stepped-up basis* is the fair market value placed on property that is purchased or inherited from another. The "step-up" refers to the increase in value from the basis of the former owner (usually what he paid for it), to the basis of the new owner (usually the market value when the transfer is made).

SUCCESSOR TRUSTEE   A *Successor Trustee* is someone who takes the place of the Trustee.

SUMMARY ADMINISTRATION   A *Summary Administration* is a simplified and/or shortened Probate procedure.

TENANCY BY THE ENTIRETY A *Tenancy by the Entirety* is a form of ownership of real property held by a husband and wife. Each person is considered to be the owner of 100% of the property both before and after the death of one of the parties. Arizona, being a Community Property state does not recognize this form of ownership.

TENANCY IN COMMON *Tenancy In Common* is a form of ownership such that each Tenant owns his share without any claim to that share by the other owners. There is no right of survivorship. Should a Tenant In Common die, his share belongs to his Estate and not to the surviving owners.

TESTATE *Testate* means having made a Will or dying with a Will.

TITLE INSURANCE *Title Insurance* is a policy issued by a title insurance company after searching title to the property. The insurance covers losses that result from a defect of title, such as unpaid taxes, or a claim of ownership of the property.

TRUST AGREEMENT A *Trust Agreement* is a document by which someone (the Settlor or Trustor) creates a Trust and appoints a Trustee to manage property placed into the Trust. The usual purpose of the Trust is to benefit persons or charities named by the Settlor as beneficiaries of the Trust.

TRUSTEE   A *Trustee* is a person, or institution, who accepts the duty of managing Trust property for the benefit of another.

UNDUE INFLUENCE   *Undue influence* is pressure, influence or persuasion that overpowers a person's free will or judgment, so that a person acts according to the will or purpose of the dominating party.

UNSECURED CREDITOR   An *unsecured creditor* is someone who is owed money on a promissory note with nothing to back it up if payment is not made. A *secured creditor* holds some special assurance of payment, such as a mortgage on real property or a lien on a car.

WAIVER   A *waiver* is the intentional and voluntary giving up of a known right.

WRONGFUL DEATH   A *wrongful death* is a death that was caused by the willful or negligent act of a person or company.

INDEX

WEB SITES

ARIZONA WEB SITES

156 Arizona Statutes are referenced in
Guiding Those Left Behind In Arizona

Each state has its own set of laws relating to the settlement of a person's Estate. The laws that are referenced in this book are very different from the laws of other states.

The author is in now in the process of "translating"
Guiding Those Left Behind
for the rest of the states, that is, writing state specific books that explain how to settle the affairs of someone who dies in the given state.

Books for the following states are now in print:
ALABAMA, ARIZONA, ARKANSAS, CALIFORNIA
CONNECTICUT, FLORIDA, GEORGIA, HAWAII, ILLINOIS
INDIANA, IOWA, KENTUCKY, LOUISIANA, MASSACHUSETTS
MARYLAND, MICHIGAN, MINNESOTA, MISSOURI
MISSISSIPPI, NEW JERSEY, NEW YORK
NORTH CAROLINA, OHIO, OKLAHOMA
PENNSYLVANIA, SOUTH CAROLINA, TENNESSEE
TEXAS, VIRGINIA, WASHINGTON, WISCONSIN

Readers of this book can purchase *Guiding Those Left Behind* for $23. This includes shipping.

To order or to check for book availability in other states call Eagle Publishing Company at (800) 824-0823.
- or -
Visit our Web site http://www.eaglepublishing.com

BOOK REVIEWS OF *Guiding Those Left Behind*

ARIZONA

Ben T. Traywick of the Tombstone Epitaph said "This book is an excellent reference book that simplifies all the necessary tasks that must be done when there is a death in the family. There is even an explanation as to how you can arrange your own estate so that your heirs will not be left with a multitude of nagging problems." "The reviewer has been going through probate for two years with no end yet in sight. This book at the beginning two year ago would have helped immensely."

CALIFORNIA

Margot Petit Nichols of the Carmel Pine Cone called it a ". . .TRULY RIVETING READ." " . . . I could scarcely put it down." "This is a book that we should all have, either on our book shelves or thoughtfully placed with our important papers."

OTHER BOOKS BY AMELIA E. POHL

Beyond Grief To Acceptance and Peace

AMELIA E. POHL and the noted psychologist BARBARA J. SIMMONDS, Ph.d, have written a book for those families who have suffered a loss.

- ✧ What to say to the bereaved
- ✧ How to help a child through the loss
- ✧ Strategies to adjust to a new life-style
- ✧ When and where to seek assistance.

80 pages   6" X 9" $10 includes Shipping and Handling
TO ORDER CALL (800) 824-0823.

A Will Is Not Enough In . . .

Many people who have a Will think that they have their affairs in order. They believe that their Will can take care of any problem that may arise. But the primary function of a Will is to distribute property to people named in a Will. A Will cannot:

⇨ Protect your assets and limit your debt

⇨ Provide care for a minor or disabled child

⇨ Avoid Guardianship

⇨ Appoint someone to make your health care decisions should you be unable to do so

⇨ Appoint someone to handle your finances should you be unable to do so

⇨ Arrange to pay for your health care should you need long term nursing care, including qualifying for MEDICAID.

AMELIA E. POHL, Esq. has written a series of state specific books explaining how to do all of these things. This new book series is a continuation of this book. It builds on basic Estate Planning concepts introduced in Chapter 7 of this book and then goes on to introduce other, more sophisticated, Estate Planning methods. Although the topics are sophisticated, the writing style is the same as in this book. It is written in plain English. It is intended for use by the average person.

A Will Is Not Enough is now available for:
ARIZONA, CALIFORNIA, CONNECTICUT, COLORADO
FLORIDA, HAWAII, INDIANA, ILLINOIS, MARYLAND
MICHIGAN, MASSACHUSETTS, NEBRASKA, NEW JERSEY
NEW MEXICO, NEW YORK, OREGON, PENNSYLVANIA
TEXAS, VIRGINIA, WASHINGTON, WISCONSIN.

Readers of this book can purchase *A Will Is Not Enough* for $25. To check for book availability in other states call Eagle Publishing Company at (800) 824-0823.

How To Defend Yourself Against Your Lawyer

is a book about the unhappy experiences people have with their lawyers, beginning with that of the author AMELIA E. POHL. She became involved in a law suit and found herself in the role of client, rather than lawyer. She become concerned about lawyers who do not provide their clients with loyalty and respect. This book is a result of those concerns.

The book is divided into chapters that cover the most common problems that take people to a lawyer: divorce, probate, criminal, personal injury, starting a business, making a Will, buying a house, etc. Each chapter tells of the misadventures of the unwary as they sought the services of a lawyer without a clue as to what they were "buying." This book is funny, sad, interesting, but most of all informative. It tells the reader how to become a savvy consumer, i.e., how to find the right lawyer for the right job. If you ever find the need to employ a lawyer, you will be glad you read this book.

Copyright 2004   272 pages 6" X 9" soft cover
$20 includes Shipping and Handling

BOOK REVIEW

TED KREITER of the SATURDAY EVENING POST said "Horror fans, forget about those tawdry tales of ghosts and vampires. Pick up Amelia E. Pohl's *How To Defend Yourself Against Your Lawyer* to read some really scary stuff. Like the story . . . of the grieving widow, Ethel, whose husband died shortly after a lawyer drafted a sweetheart will for the two of them. . . . Six months in attorney's fees later, Ethel learned that she already had her husband's money because it never needed to go through probate! . . Ethel then went out and found a good lawyer for $1,000 who was able to get her $5,000 back. You do the math. . . Following Pohl's useful advice could save a person much more than money."

It is the goal of EAGLE PUBLISHING COMPANY to keep our publications fresh.

As we receive information about changes to the federal or state law we will post an update to this edition at our Web site.

http://www.eaglepublishing.com